monsoonbooks

G000229919

SOLD FOR SILVER

Janet Lim lived in Singapore, Malaysia and Hong Kong before settling permanently in Queensland, Australia, where she has three children and six grandsons.

Twenty years after WWII, doctors discovered that Janet had suffered a ruptured spleen and bowel from jumping into the sea when the ship she was escaping Singapore on was bombed and sunk by the Japanese. That she did not succumb to her internal injuries during her two-day ordeal drifting at sea, Janet ascribes to God and salt water.

Acclaim for *Sold for Silver*

"Singapore slave's tale a bestseller. Three TV networks vying for rights to Janet Lim's book" *Streats*

"… a historically important and inspirational story … what will strike you about this book is the lack of bitterness in her account." *The Straits Times*

"Readers will quickly get caught up in this fascinating narrative … [a] compelling story of endurance, faith and friendship." *Publishers Weekly*

"… despite the events of her life, Lim is cheerful and her life philosophy is inspiring in its simplicity." *TODAY*

"A vivid and true account of one's brush with slavery, *Sold for Silver* is a beautiful and poignant read." *Think*

"*Sold for Silver* is an inspiration. A pin-prick of light when all is dark." *New Straits Times*

Sold for Silver

An Autobiography of a Girl Sold into Slavery in Southeast Asia

Janet Lim

monsoon

monsoonbooks

Published in 2004
by Monsoon Books Pte Ltd
Blk 106 Jalan Hang Jebat #02–14
Singapore 139527
www.monsoonbooks.com.sg

First published in 1958
by William Collins & Sons, UK

ISBN-13: 978-981-05-1728-1
ISBN-10: 981-05-1728-9

Part of the proceeds from the sale of this book will be
given by the author and publisher to charity.

Front-cover photograph: Ah Moy, a *mui tsai* (child slave)
from Hong Kong, *c*. 1930 (©Anti-Slavery International)

Printed in Singapore

09 08 07 06 05   2 3 4 5 6 7 8 9

For my grandsons
Matthew, Andrew, David, Mark, Adam and Daniel

Contents

Foreword

There will probably be two types of readers of this autobiography. Some will find in its pages a romance of the East, and may be moved by Miss Lim's trials and rejoice with her at the final happy outcome of her remarkable adventures. These readers may be glad of my assurance that the story is a true account. They may be disappointed not to hear of the post-war years, when the heroine reached a position of responsibility and leadership both in her profession of nursing and in her work for the Church of God. After finishing her nursing training, which had been interrupted by the war, Miss Lim rejoined the staff of St Andrew's Mission Hospital in 1948, becoming its first Asian Matron in 1954. In addition, she has travelled widely; she has had periods of postgraduate study in the U.K. and Australia, and has visited much of Asia.

I venture to think that a greater number will be those who are looking for some sense of reality in a much disturbed world. Those who have had experience of the pursuit of aims of their own, will find great satisfaction and inspiration in these pages.

My own knowledge of the writer goes back to her entry into the Church of England Zenana Missionary Society School in Singapore. My clearest recollection of her is on the day of her baptism when I called on a large-eyed little girl to make her Christian vows. But I had known her before that, for my wife was concerned with the Poh Leung Kuk Home, and had to do with the decision to allow her to go to an English school. At that time little Janet already had a reputation of restlessly seeking for something that she called a "Jesus School". Her arrival at the school at Sophia Road, Singapore, was long remembered. For the child it was the end of a long quest and the beginning of a new life.

R.K. Sorby Adams, 1958

Early Childhood
1923–1932

"Singapore!" someone shouted, and I looked across the wharf. There were men working, but they looked different from any I had ever seen. Their bodies were dark and they were chewing something red; they dressed differently too, wearing only some pieces of cloth around the lower parts of their bodies. They spoke a language I could not understand. Tears rolled down my cheeks as I realised that Singapore was very far from China. When my father was alive he had told me stories about it, and I remembered that he had taught me two Malay words—"*makan*" (to eat) and "*tangkap*" (to catch). He had told me also that little girls went to school in Singapore, adding, "When you are big, Chiu Mei, I will send you to school."

My thoughts were interrupted by the woman beside me saying, "Remember what I told you." Yes, I would remember! Like my other child companions, I had been told that I must tell anyone who questioned me that this woman was my aunt. Soon we were clear of the customs and were taken to a *kampung* (village) where we were ordered to walk up and down. Someone pointed to me and said, "She would be worth more if her nose were not so flat." I understood a word here and there and realised to my horror that I was going to be sold!

That night there were seven of us left, five girls and two little boys who were, I was told, sons of our "aunt" though they were treated no better than we were. By and by the other girls disappeared; finally only

11

two of us were left. I thought that my flat nose was going to save me. My companion looked at me inquiringly; but how could I, a girl of eight, explain anything to her? We were both frightened of the future. Soon she knew her fate, for she left two days earlier than I.

When my turn came I was taken to see a kind though very untidy-looking woman. That night I stayed with her, and was told to sleep under her bed; but sleep was very far away. I could not stop thinking of my home in China, a very happy home, but one which I had known for only a short period.

I was born in Hong Kong on the first day of the sixth moon of the Year of the Pig, according to Chinese reckoning. The Chinese calendar runs in cycles of sixty years. Each year is distinguished by two characters, one a Celestial Stem signifying one of the ten planets, the other a Terrestrial Branch representing one of twelve animals. The ten Celestial Stems and the twelve Terrestrial Branches rotate in a regular sequence and, as the lowest common multiple of ten and twelve is sixty, the cycle recurs every sixty years. The first cycle started in 2697 BC with the reign of Emperor Huang Ti and the same reckoning has continued ever since; I was born in the last year of the 77th cycle—14 July 1923. My father called me Chiu Mei (Autumn Beauty) because it was a time of the year which he loved very much. I fear that the second part of my name is hardly appropriate!

My father was a *sin seh* (doctor). He practised according to the traditional Chinese medical system for as far as I know he had had no Western training. His family's home was on the mainland of China. There he had rice fields and plantations of sugar cane and groundnuts. My father was about ten years older than my mother. They had been married when my mother was thirteen years of age—a marriage arranged by her parents. In China in those days, it was considered scandalous for a man to see his betrothed before the wedding day.

However, my father did not want to find himself married to a blind or deformed wife, so he arranged with the matchmaker to have a secret glimpse of his future bride. The matchmaker told my father to disguise himself as a vegetable hawker; in this way he was able to get within a few yards of her while she was playing with some of her friends. He carried his load of vegetables clumsily, calling out *"Boey cha ya"* (vegetables for sale), but his head was turned towards the girls. Soon people noticed this unusual hawker and the news reached the girl's relations. Afterwards my father had to apologise and nearly lost his bride. Besides, the plan had been a disappointment for he had failed to identify his betrothed from among the other children. For a long time the village elders frowned severely on him for his undignified behaviour.

I must have been a few months old when my parents decided to leave Hong Kong and make a home in China; perhaps my father wanted to be near his estate. It was in his home village that my brother and my two sisters were born. My eldest sister I remember only vaguely; she was never named. Soon after her birth she was given away to a convent because of a prediction by the gods that if she lived at home I should die. She herself died in early infancy in the convent. My brother was born a year later and my parents were very happy. I remember that there was great rejoicing at the "bathing ceremony" held in celebration of his reaching the age of one month. Mother prepared a bath in the centre of the room and dropped two boiled eggs into the water and Father shaved my brother's hair. Afterwards, hundreds of eggs were distributed to relations and friends.

My brother was a very intelligent boy and though he was much younger than I, he always seemed to know how to say the right thing at the right time. At weddings he was always ready with his good wishes— "Long life and many sons"—whereas I stood behind with open lips through which no words came.

My second sister was about four years younger than my brother. I remember we were having dinner when Mother left to prepare her room. In the village all mothers delivered their own babies. The floor was covered with paper and a low stool was placed in front of her bed so that she could sit during delivery, resting her back against the bed. She then left the kettle to boil, lit the lamp in her room and washed up our dinner things. Father and I shared a bed in another room; we jumped up when we heard a baby's cry. Then we rushed into Mother's room and found a tiny pink object on the floor. I was thrilled as I had never seen such a small baby before. Mother mopped up the floor while Father prepared the bath. The next morning Mother was up and about doing her usual work; there was no fuss. Alas! My poor sister also died soon after birth. I have often wondered whether, had she lived, she would have shared my fate. Perhaps it was as well she died young.

Our house, like many other Chinese houses in the village, had dragons over the doorway. A person entering it came at once into a large hall, which was used for visitors, for family recreation and for meals. On the left were several bedrooms leading off the main hall, my father and I occupying one of them and my mother and brother another. On the right of the hall was the kitchen. Its door was oval and rather low, so that Father had to stoop as he went in—a thing he seldom did as the kitchen was a place for women only. The house stood in the main street of the village, the front being right on the road and it was here that we children always played. On the other side was a row of houses, but directly opposite was an open place closed in by a low wall. I think this was done because of some superstition which said that if one house faced another, the people living in these houses would oppose one another.

One end of the street led to a wooded park. In it stood the village church which my father had been mainly instrumental in building. He was a devout Roman Catholic though my mother was a Buddhist. About once a month a European priest came on horseback and I remember our amazement at his strange white colour, his high nose and fair hair. The occasion was celebrated by a feast which took place outside the church after the service. This priest was the only European I can remember seeing during my childhood, except for a party who one day caused great excitement in the village. I have no idea who they were or where they came from, but we children suddenly found a number of tired-looking men resting under a tree. We stood at a distance, too afraid to go near because we had often been warned that strangers kidnapped children and cut them up for medicine. But the men smiled and waved to us and soon we were stroking their white hairy arms and examining their watches—things we had never seen. Later I heard that these men were Christians who had come to destroy our temples. To show us that the idols were made by men and were powerless, they threw them into the drain, an action which caused consternation and resentment amongst the villagers.

At the other end of the village the street widened into an open space which was used for public events, such as meetings and funerals. More important still, it contained the village well. In summer, when there was a drought, hundreds of people waited beside this well to get water and every drop was scooped up. It stood about a quarter of a mile from our house and carrying the water was a daily task which we all shared. The village was surrounded by a great wall with four gates which were opened only from sunrise to sunset. We got almost all our produce from land outside the wall; inside only some vegetables and some fruit were grown.

My father's property supplied most of our vegetables, such as beans and sweet potatoes; the latter was our main food. Rice was grown for export. We only ate it on special occasions, like Chinese New Year, or if we were sick. I often used to follow my father to the plantation and give him what little help I could. Locusts were our worst pests; to destroy them we poured kerosene around each plant. It was a tedious task and I often fell asleep between the vegetable beds. When Father found me he never scolded me but took me up in his arms and whispered that the day's work was finished and that we were going home. On the way he would stop at various places to look for herbs for the patients who were waiting for him. His only free time was in the evenings; when he did not spend it with us he went to the Judo Club. Most of the members of the club idled the time away gambling but although it was the most popular pastime in the village my father disliked gambling exceedingly. There were no other amusements; cinemas were unheard of. I remember how surprised my mother and I were when we first heard a gramophone; we wanted to know where the singer was, so we turned the gramophone upside down, and thereby broke the precious record.

Women were mainly occupied in housework, though some helped in the plantation. There were no servants except during the harvest; then help was needed because of the large meals which were required for the labourers. Whenever Mother was free she went to her friend next door and gossiped about domestic events. Chinese wives lived almost entirely separated from their husbands. It was considered vulgar for a wife to look at her husband or to be seen with him in public. My mother was no exception to this convention. I cannot ever remember seeing her go out with my father; such behaviour would have been too modern for our village. She seldom went beyond the high walls of the village except to visit her parents who lived in the next village; on these visits I usually accompanied her. Quarrels among the women were common, and generally arose out of their children's fights. My mother disliked these quarrels so if I was involved I got a beating, for she believed that it was better to discipline one's child than to quarrel with one's neighbours.

A village girl enjoyed great freedom before her marriage; but after a marriage had been arranged she was strictly forbidden to go out alone. Once I accompanied my father to my cousin's wedding. During the wedding feast I sat with the other children and I remember that my uncle insisted that I should eat the carrots which were being served. I burst out crying because I disliked carrots. My uncle and aunt were furious for they believed that it was most unlucky to cry on such an occasion. Three months later my cousin's wife hanged herself and I was blamed!

Most of the village girls were taught at an early age to do housework. Cooking, sewing and looking after the house formed a girl's passport to marriage and some strict prospective mothers-in-law insisted on investigating a girl's work before they would accept her. When I was six years old I went to an embroidery class, mainly, I think, to fill in the time. Some afternoons when my mother allowed it, I joined the other children in flying kites, which was our favourite game. In the evenings our parents watched the races and the singing competitions which were held near our home. It was not unusual to see children gambling. I once joined in a gambling game, and lost one cent. As I was not given any pocket money, I stole the cent from a box in which odd cash was kept, hoping that one cent would not be missed. The discovery of the loss resulted in Mother giving me a caning. She also refused to let me have my evening meal and pushed me out of the house and shut the door in my face. I cried myself to sleep on the doorstep. It was dark when my father returned and found me. He was furious. This was the only time I can remember my father and mother quarrelling.

My mother, like most village women, was convinced that daughters were of little value. Once they were fifteen, the age at which they were most useful in the home, they were married off and contact was then lost with them, for their allegiance was thereafter given to their husband's family. Mother was a very strict woman and never showed her love for me. Nor did she answer my endless questions; instead, I received slaps on the face for being too talkative. Though I loved her I did not dare to show lily feelings and any signs of affection between us were unknown. My mother often complained that I was the ugliest child in the family. This worried me so much that I looked in the mirror and smeared my face with soap thinking it would make me beautiful. My father, on the other hand, was very gentle, patient and affectionate and I used to jump on to his knee and hug him. Except in the evenings, we did not see a great deal of him. These hours with my father, however, are amongst my most cherished memories. He often took me for walks, and he told me stories, mostly about animals, some of which I can still remember. I can see him now with his long hair coiled around his head, smoking a long pipe, at intervals knocking out the ash into a multicoloured Chinese bowl which stood on the table.

Occasionally the regular routine of the village was interrupted by exciting events. I remember a war between my maternal grandmother's village and ours. The fight started over the ownership of a piece of land. The men of our village spent the whole night preparing weapons— home-made hand-grenades and swords. My parents were in a very difficult situation because if they helped our village they would be fighting against their own relations. So they made up their minds that they would not help either side. They were reassured when my mother received a message from her brother saying that he would protect our home if our village lost the war. The fight went on for two days; our men spent most of the time behind the village wall! Someone told my mother that her father had been seen outside our village gate trying to stop the fighting but that no one would listen to him, and that he had been stoned. My mother gave me a knife and told me to kill anyone who tried to enter our home. I was so frightened that I looked at the knife with terror and did not know which god to turn to—my mother's or my father's! In the end the fight was settled by the village elders, and both sides carried their wounded inside the walls; I am not sure which side won. After that we were not on speaking terms with the people of the enemy village; even we children would not speak to the children of the other side. I remember that I quarrelled with a little boy who was on the other bank of the lake which separated the two villages. I did not know then that he was a close relation. I learnt this fact, to my great shame, when I later visited his home with Mother.

My parents had four pigs which I bathed twice a day. The neighbours were most amused as I washed them very thoroughly with soap, a scrubbing brush and a towel. As in many homes in the villages, our pigs had the freedom of the house. After their bath they wandered out into the village but always came home in time for their dinner. During the night they would wake me up if they wanted to go outside to relieve themselves. I remember my parents saying that if it had not been for the pigs and the noise they made, we would have been devoured by wolves. In summer, we usually slept with the doors wide open. One night the pigs made a great noise and Father got out of bed to investigate; to his horror he saw a large wolf in our sitting room. He got hold of a tin and the noise he made drove the wolf away.

Two of my cousins were killed by wolves. One was four years old and was watching his mother feeding the pigs at dusk, when a wolf snatched him away unknown to his mother. When she realised what had happened, she took a lamp and went up the hill to look for her son but she only found two of his fingers. The other cousin was twelve years old. He was told by his father to carry a watering-can and some planting tools to a nearby farm. He must have been seized as soon as he reached the farm. The tracks of the wolf were easily followed; grass and plants had been torn up for, as he was being dragged along, the child had grasped at anything within reach. A couple of men had actually seen two wolves feeding but they had supposed they were eating a pig.

I too had an experience with wolves. We were harvesting the groundnuts one evening, when I forgot a cooking pot which I had been told to bring home. I was afraid to tell Mother I had been careless, so I left the house very early next morning for the plantation. When I got there I noticed a dog fight, but did not realise that the dogs were fighting wolves. I came within a few yards of them; then an animal ran towards me and, to my horror, I noticed its huge wide mouth. Luckily there was a tree nearby. I had learned my lesson and I never went out early again.

The temples also remain in my memory—I remember one which I visited while I was staying at a large village. It was during the seventh moon feast, and every household had contributed some gift towards the celebrations. Many large stands and paper statues were put up, together with a host of images. Our villages offered sacrifices to the ghosts—to the hungry ones, those who had died without leaving any relations behind who would offer them food. The villagers believed that these hungry ghosts were allowed to leave the spirit world once a year and that then they wandered at large in search of offerings. We children had a gay time as there were free stage shows at this season. It was during such a celebration that one of my friends decided we should visit some famous temples in the village. I remember that we slipped in unnoticed and joined a group of visitors. The caretaker explained the presence of a set of wedding furniture which was to be seen in the temple. It seemed that a young girl who was going to be married had been told by her parents to go to the temple to thank the god. She did not like the idea of going by herself so she took her sister-in-law with her. After burning the joss-sticks, they had a look around the temple and the sister-in-law pointed to one of the gods and remarked, "How handsome he is. I hope your husband will be like him." No sooner had she stopped talking than the girl twisted her ankle. They returned home but the future bride fell ill and the parents believed that both the girls had offended the god. The girl's mother immediately went to the temple and thought she saw her daughter sitting with the god; on her return to the house she found her daughter dead. The mother was then convinced that the girl had been chosen by the god and it was for this reason that she sent all her wedding furniture to the temple. One of the visitors asked why there was a bath-tub in the room. We were told that after the room was furnished, the girl's parents hired a servant to look after it and she used the tub to prepare baths.

The feast of the seventh moon passed and other festivals came and went. My home was indeed a happy place, but only for a few years. I can remember my parents' grief when they told me that my brother, now four years of age, was very ill. It was summer and my mother could not find a spot cool enough in the house for him to sleep in, so she decided to let him rest at times in the wooded park which faced our village church. One day he woke up, and finding no one near him, gathered up his pillow and mat and walked slowly home. He stood in the outer hall facing me and I can still see his thin, wasted body—it was so shocking that I wanted to run away. My mother rushed out and gathered him up in her arms, exclaiming, "What a clever boy you are! Though you are so ill you can still think of bringing your things home with you." Many an hour she spent beside his bed, sometimes the whole night. He died early one morning and I saw his still body laid out on the floor, cold and white. Someone told me that he had gone to a better land.

"I'll see him next week," I thought. Death conveyed little to me; I only missed a playmate. Then a tiny coffin arrived. My brother was dressed in three layers of clothing. The fronts of his shirts were ripped into ribbons, for my mother believed that if his shirts had no holes in them he would have to carry sand and help to build bridges in the next world. If there had been other boys in the family, perhaps my parents would not have been so grieved, but it was a terrible blow to lose their only son.

Soon after my brother's death, my father's health began to fail. I did not know then what he was suffering from, but he had a cough and lost his voice; looking back, I think that he probably had tuberculosis. Now I began to wonder why my brother had been absent for so long, and the thought that my father might also go away terrified me. One day I remember looking at him for a long time and saying, "Papa, you must not also go away." He hugged me without saying a word and I remember that there were tears in his eyes.

After the death of my brother and of my second sister, life became very lonely for my parents for I was the only child left. My father had no relations living near. His parents had died when he was very young and his only sister had married and lived far away. He had a brother in Singapore but my mother and I did not know of this until he was dying, when he told us about him. As the weeks went on my father became weaker and had to be helped to go about. My mother and I wrapped him in blankets because he felt the cold. He liked to sit outside the door of the house to watch the passers-by and have a few words with his friends. Perhaps he realised that he was going to die for I remember hearing him talking to Mother, advising her how and when to plant certain crops. As I look back now, I think that my father must have loved me very much. I remember an evening when I returned shivering because my clothes were wet; even though he was so weak, he staggered out of bed to help me change. I cannot remember him scolding me, except on one occasion when he had repeatedly told me that I was not to drink out of his teacup.

One day about noon, Mother told me in hushed tones and with eyes filled with tears, that I must go and sit near Father. Her sad face brought back the memory of my brother's death and I hurried to my father's side. A mat had been placed on the floor, with a layer of hay beneath it for warmth. My father was lying on this, covered by a few blankets. Mother and I sat beside him the whole day. When evening came he knew he was dying; he held my hands and looked at Mother and said, "Look after Chiu Mei." Then he talked to my mother about the estate, telling her not to worry about it because he had a brother in Singapore. My father firmly believed in a life after death and he must have thought that after he had died he would be able to make contact with his brother. He said so to my mother: "When I am gone, I will go to Singapore to my brother; he will help you with the estate." He indicated that he did not wish my mother to remarry, but that, according to Chinese custom, he would prefer her to adopt a son to carry on the family name. During the evening he lapsed into unconsciousness. He rallied a few times, then he died at three o'clock in the morning.

Even though it was still dark, my mother told me to go and report the death to the village elder. When I returned, I remember lying down beside my father and I think that I must have gone off to sleep. The funeral took place three days later, and I still regret that I did not follow the procession to the burial ground. So, by the age of six, I had seen three deaths in my family. I could not believe that I should never see my father again, and little did I realise then that his death would change my whole life.

After the death of my father, my mother and her friends looked after the plantation. But in China, women were not entitled to inherit property; everything went to sons or, if there were no sons, to brothers or to nephews. During my childhood, various laws were introduced which changed this system of inheritance to one nearer to the Western type and enabled property to pass to widows and to female children, but when my father died the old laws still survived in the villages. Whether my father was influenced by the new ideas I do not know, but it appears that he willed the whole estate to me.

One morning Mother left the house early with a friend, to go to the market. This was a whole day's journey by foot and there was no other means of transport. Soon after Mother's departure, I went to the back room of the house and had a good feed from two sacks of lychees which were meant for export. Then, suddenly, I heard noises outside the house. I peeped through the keyhole and saw a group of men. I thought that they had come to buy our pigs, from which I could not bear to be parted. Then among them I noticed a tall man, who was the image of my father, so I lost no time in opening the door. But the tall man did not pay any attention to me.

"He cannot be my papa," I thought. "If he were, he would have taken me up in his arms."

Then someone said to me, "Chiu Mei, this is your uncle who has just come from Singapore."

The tall man looked at me and smiled, but I was afraid, seeing so many men in the house. Except for a playmate, I was alone and my first thought was for the pigs. "Whatever happens, no one must harm my pigs." I stood guarding them until the men left. In the evening my mother returned and I told her all that had happened. She was not surprised that Uncle had come home, but his coming must have accentuated her sense of loss, for she was terribly upset, and between her sobs she quoted the Chinese saying, "You can go far away from home, but you can always return; once you are dead, there is no return."

Soon Uncle reappeared. He told Mother he had made up his mind never to come back to China, but suddenly one morning he had decided to do so. Here and there I gathered a word or two, and I could see that Mother found it difficult to get on with my uncle. Probably they were arguing over the ownership of the estate. My uncle stayed on and as the weeks went by there were frequent quarrels between them, which terrified me. To make things worse, my uncle was mixing with bad company and had begun to sell part of the estate. Then one day there was a big fight which resulted in Mother receiving a large cut on her face. I was so angry that I crouched between them and bit my uncle on the leg. I remember that we had to walk miles to a police station and that after making a statement we went to stay with friends. The next day we went back to the police station and this time my uncle was there too. The police asked me questions about him, but somehow I could not tell them the truth because he looked so like Father. Uncle was sent to jail. In those days jails in China were horrible places, and after seeing Uncle in jail I could not help feeling sorry for him. After a short time in prison, he returned and the arguments about the estate began again and finally a village meeting was held. We drew lots in public in the presence of the village elders. I was too young to understand what had been decided, though I remember that there were loud cheers from the whole village. As far as I know Mother and I were to keep the house, where, in fact, we continued to live, but I cannot remember any details about the division of the estate.

After this Mother was never again the same person. We continued nightly prayers for Father's soul; I never liked these prayers because, after the people had gone, Mother always cried and I could not bear to see her so unhappy. I too was unhappy for Father was my hero. Mother never talked to me as parents do today to children. I spent hours at the graves of my father and of my brother—there I understood the meaning of the word dead.

So the months dragged on till the following year. Then one morning Mother got up early. She had spent the whole night weeping and her eyes were red and swollen. When I woke up she was extremely kind to me; she asked me what I would like to eat, brought out my favourite clothes, combed my hair and dressed me. I felt that something was wrong—perhaps she was going to join my father, a thing she often threatened to do. After breakfast, she told me to go to my grandmother's house to bring her back to our home. Mother walked with me to the main road, weeping all the way, but when she had disappeared I did not go to Grandmother's but wandered up the hill. It must have been about noon when I reached Father's grave. There I became hysterical, beat on the tombstone and shouted to Father to come home. The grave was near the main road and many people who were passing by came over to look at me; those who could read knew it was my father's grave and said, "Poor child! Have you nobody to look after you?" The next thing I remember was that the sun was setting and I realised that I was very far from home, but I could not make up my mind whether to return or not. Supposing Mother was dead when I got home? This idea grieved me. Mother had expected me to be away for about an hour and then to bring Grandmother back. She told me afterwards that she had intended first to hand over all the money and jewellery to Grandmother for my upkeep and then to kill herself, but while she was waiting, two large butterflies appeared. My mother, like so many village people, believed that butterflies represented the dead, and somehow or other she felt that she could not commit suicide until she had seen me again. When I returned it was already night, I was dirty, my face and eyes were swollen. I had not eaten anything all day and I was very exhausted.

She was very gentle and asked me, "Where have you been, Chiu Mei?"

With eyes full of tears I told her, "I got to Grandma's house but the door was shut so I waited outside and I went to sleep."

Even Grandmother, who tried later to get the truth out of me, failed.

Before I had finished talking, I fainted and afterwards became ill. I lost consciousness for some days during which many people visited me. Mother went to a soothsayer who said that if I didn't regain consciousness by the first or second day of the sixth moon I would never wake up again. I remember that when I opened my eyes I saw that I had on one of my prettiest Chinese dresses, and it seemed to me that I had woken from a dream. I was very weak.

Gradually I regained my strength but when I was well enough to go out and look for my friends, no one would play with me. They were afraid of me, saying that since I had come back from the dead, I must now be a spirit or a ghost, which made me wonder if I was one! But I did not care. Because of what I had gone through, I seemed to have lost all pleasure in children's games and so I decided I must grow up soon. Even Mother saw the change in me.

In summer, especially on moonlight nights, most people sat out of doors till very late. The children played or sang but I seldom joined in. Instead, I would stay indoors and pretend to be asleep so that I could listen to Mother's conversation. In this way I learned many things.

One night someone said to Mother, "You treat your daughter in such a way that no one believes she is yours."

I was very grateful when she said, "I love Chiu Mei more than you love your son; my love is like a pearl deep in the sea."

I did not know what she meant by the pearl deep in the sea, but it was enough for me that Mother loved me. I was always afraid in case anything should happen to her, for then I should be all alone in the world; I was always careful not to anger her. At times when she was not well I would pray secretly, calling to Father who had taught me to pray. My religion was very mixed at this time. Mother was a Buddhist, and whenever I was sick she would wrap me up in a pair of black trousers and send me to a temple to sit under Buddha's large feet, so that the evil spirit which had caused my illness should leave me. I was terrified of Buddha, and I always believed that he might strike me. Sometimes I spent hours in the temple.

One day Mother started packing and a man, a friend of Father's, arrived. I was told that we were going for a long journey, and I was very grieved when I wasn't allowed to take my cat with me. However, we started on that long journey, climbing over hills and mountains, passing bandits and crossing rivers, all the way on foot, I was so tired that I cried out that I could not walk; Mother too had very sore feet. We slept in the open air. All this seemed like a nightmare; I do not know how long it took us to get to our destination but it seemed years to me. I did not know to what district we were heading; I just followed and asked no questions. Finally we arrived at a large town which had fruit trees everywhere. We were housed in a big place full of women and children and I was told I must not go out by myself. I thought that life in this place was unbearable; I longed for familiar faces—Mother's alone was not enough. I used to choose a lonely place, under a tree or near a rock, and think of my friends and my father and my cat. I felt lost and unwanted. One evening Mother found me there and she was very upset and wanted to know why I hid myself away every evening, but I could not explain.

One morning I saw all the women, including Mother, dressed up in their best clothes. They walked round the garden twice, and, to my great dismay, I noticed that there were a few men looking at them. Then there was a feast and later that evening I was introduced to a man. Someone told me he was to be my father. I was appalled! How could I have two fathers? I refused to eat and howled.

For the first four months of her second marriage, Mother shared a room with me. I suppose this was intended to get me used to my step-father, whom I called "Uncle." We lived with the family, my stepfather's father, two widowed sisters-in-law, two nephews and a niece. My stepfather's eldest sister-in-law was a very hard woman; I thought she had a face like a horse, and she always stared at me with her piercing eyes. I disliked her intensely but dared not show it. His second sister-in-law was slightly built and had a kind face. I was upset when I was told to call this woman "Mother". I was very muddled since no one had explained to me why all of a sudden I had a new father and now had to call someone else Mother. I hated myself and everybody around me. Often I would wander far out into the country and find a lonely place, not to cry in, but to think in, for I had already vowed to myself that I was a grown-up girl, so I would not cry. I saw the hardships Mother had to endure as a newcomer to this house and I resented everybody, including my stepfather. He often tried to make friends with me; but I could not bear to think that he was taking my father's place. I even told him that we were not related to each other.

"The two of us have different surnames. How can we be related?" I asked.

As a bride, Mother had to serve everybody at meal times, and according to custom for four months she was not allowed to sit down for her own meals. One evening as I wandered round the country I saw my stepfather's youngest nephew carrying a bundle of firewood. I went over to help him but he refused, and stared at me as though I were a ghost. I ran all the way home, feeling very ashamed of myself and asked Mother why everybody disliked me. Then for the first time it dawned on me that this boy, who was about my age, was going to be my husband, and this explained his shyness on seeing me, since, by Chinese custom, engaged couples, even children, never talked together in public. This also explained why I had to call his mother "Mother".

I got on very well with my new grandfather, in fact I became his favourite granddaughter, and, as the weeks went by, I spent more time with him than with anyone else. I remember there was a drought and there was no water for the paddy or for the vegetable fields. Everybody went out to dig for water, for we had no rice to eat. It seemed to me that everyone was starving except Grandfather and myself; he had a little stove in his office where he did all his cooking and shared his food with me.

When Mother no longer shared her room with me, I stayed at night with a neighbour. One evening my stepfather told me to sleep in the hall and that at midnight Mother would wake me up; I was not to make a noise but to follow them. I was very curious and could not sleep. I understood later that both of them, especially my mother, were very unhappy in the clan home and had decided to leave it secretly. At midnight Mother woke me. "Chiu Mei, put this on," she said, handing me a coat. Then I followed her and my stepfather into the darkness. We walked and walked and it seemed to me the road was never going to end, but at last we came to a friend's house and had something to eat; and then we went on walking again. Soon I recognised the road—it was the road to my own village, from which we had travelled some months before in the opposite direction. I looked at the man walking beside us, and thought of how we had had Father's friend with us on our previous journey. Why had he taken Mother and me to this far district to marry us off? Even today this puzzles me. I do not remember very much of this journey; it was uneventful. But as we went we helped ourselves to the fruit that grew plentifully by the roadside.

After several days, we arrived, very late one evening, at my maternal grandmother's house. The street lights were lit up and everybody shouted "Welcome home."

I could not express my joy at seeing my family again.

Grandfather looked at me. "Chiu Mei, you have grown. You are taller and you look older."

The next morning at breakfast I had two eggs dyed red and a bowl of sweet noodles. It was my birthday (July 1931)—I was eight years old. At that time I could not know that it would be the last birthday that my mother would celebrate with me. We stayed in the village for about a week, then we went on again. As we were leaving, I realised, as if by instinct, that this was to be the last time I would see my family. When I said goodbye I thought my heart was going to break. Grandfather silently carried our few belongings and almost the whole village turned out to see us off.

We left when the sun was setting and after a short distance we took a boat. It was the first time that I had been in a boat; I was seasick and so was Mother. The journey took one night and we arrived early the next morning at Swatow. I had never before seen rickshaws or motor cars and they fascinated me. We stayed first in a house which was full of people and very dirty; later we moved to a high building with endless steps. During the day I helped a family who had a stall to sell sweets. I had no idea who this family was, but there was talk about the son of this family becoming engaged to me. The idea of becoming engaged or of being married conveyed very little to me then, but I remembered a cousin of mine who had been married; his wife who was very young had become a great friend of mine. One morning she told me, "You know, Chiu Mei, I found a man in my room last night and I fought him and this morning I got a scolding from my mother-in-law." She told me that she often spent a lot of time hiding up the chimney because of this man.

As the months went by, I became more friendly with my stepfather, but I still could not think of him as my father. On the whole we were happy in Swatow, but my stepfather was very restless. He had failed to find work, and talked of returning home. I was anxious when I thought of my step-grandfather: he had been so good to me, and yet I had run away at midnight without even saying goodbye to him! What would he think of me? Nor did I like the idea of meeting the rest of my stepfather's family because they had been very cold towards me.

Finally it was decided that we should leave Swatow and, after saying goodbye to the family we were staying with, we left by train. I was told that we were going to a nearby town where I was to be left with a friend who would take care of me while my parents returned to my stepfather's home. The journey was considered too tiring for me and indeed our earlier journey had been a terrible ordeal. My parents said that they would come back for me in about three months' time. At first I accepted the plan but, when I thought it over, three months without Mother seemed beyond endurance. I said that I could not stand it and protested, but they won in the end.

We came to a huge house belonging to a wealthy family and remained with them for a few days. Then came the morning, the morning which will always live in my memory, when Mother gave me twenty-five cents and told me to be good and promised that they would soon come back for me. I followed my stepfather and my mother to the door and across the courtyard; then, with tears rolling down my cheeks, I watched them go, their figures getting smaller and smaller till they disappeared out of my sight. That was the last I ever saw of them.

In my new home I was most miserable for it was the first time I had been separated from Mother. I could not sleep or eat but counted the days till I would see her again. They seemed very long as I had no particular duties, so one night, after I had been there for about a month, I planned to run away and find a friend in Swatow who would help me to return home. I had to see Mother. "I must, I must see her." The next morning I got up, before anyone was awake, and slipped out of the house unnoticed. Once outside the gate I ran. It was still dark but I followed the railway line which would, I hoped, lead me to Swatow. Exhausted though I was, I dared not stop to breathe, but ran on and on, and my hopes rose high when far away I saw the gate of Swatow. In twenty minutes I would be safely there and once inside the gate I knew that it would be difficult to find me. But then I heard a train coming, and as I was in the middle of the track I had to stand aside to let it pass. A man looked out of a carriage window and saw me; later he told me that his gods had helped him. I cursed his gods. He must have got out of the train at the next stop because soon after that he came towards me. This was a great shock to me after all my careful planning. He gripped me tightly; I struggled and bit his hands. In front of me was a river in which the water ran fiercely. I tried to jump into it, but the man was too strong for me, so I gave up and was brought back to the family. I had never seen the mistress so savage before; she was like a tigress, she sprang at me and shouted that I was an ungrateful dog. She got hold of my hair and flung me to the floor. She sat on my stomach and pinched my body between her great long fingernails. They sank deeply into my flesh. The man who had brought me back kept on saying, "That's enough." But it was not enough to satisfy this fierce woman. I must have fainted, for the next thing I remember is waking up to find myself chained to a door and there I remained chained for a month. I was treated like a dog and like a dog I behaved. I begged on my knees for food, to be taken to the latrine or for a wash; sometimes my requests were granted, but generally no attention was paid to me. The other children laughed at me and made fun of me.

I won my freedom in a curious way. A neighbouring woman, who was able to go into a trance and contact the spirits of the dead, happened to be the main topic of conversation in the house. I saw my chance and boldly told the mistress that I knew all about the spirits. She was interested so I told her that just before Father died we had celebrated the eighth moon. This is the month in which most people "invite the spirits". An old Chinese legend tells of two quarrelling sisters-in-law and of how one strangled the other. Not knowing what to do with the body she hid it in the drain. (In Chinese houses drains run from the kitchen to the outside.) Through the spirit of this dead sister-in-law it was believed that one could get into touch with the spirits of one's relations and friends. I said to my mistress that I had seen this done. She was very superstitious and was so impressed that she believed that I was one of these mediums. In this way my bluffing won me my freedom. Now I was allowed to eat my meals like the other children; in fact, I was given special privileges.

A fortnight later I was told that since I had been a good girl I was going home. I was overjoyed; I was so happy that I cried. We embarked at Swatow. I remained in my happy dream for several days, then I discovered that I was not going home. But even then I did not know where we were going. A week later someone shouted, "Singapore!"

A Slave Girl
1932–1934

I was looked at, criticised, and after much bargaining, sold for $250. My master was an old man. Living with him was his second wife, who had been his former servant, and their son, who was about my age. His first wife, who had several grown-up children, lived about five miles away. In our house there were also two servants and two other girls, one a slave like myself and the other a distant relation. I soon learnt that a servant had a higher status than a slave; because the slave had been purchased, the master could do whatever he pleased with her. My outlook changed; I no longer looked forward to the days ahead, but moved about like a machine. I envied the happy little girls, secure in their mother's love, who often visited the family. I, a slave, dared not even approach them, much less play with them, because we were not equals.

Mostly I was given housework to do. I had also to look after the poultry. This I did not mind; indeed the geese were my great friends. I talked to them about my sorrows and worries, and, turning their heads this way and that, they seemed to understand me. It was in this household that I learned to cook, sew and swear! I had no friends except the geese and although the other slave was my equal, we had little to do with each other, for she was the mistress's favourite. I was very lonely, and after my day's work I would go into the garden to be comforted by my friends, the geese. The time went by slowly and painfully; every day I hoped that I might meet my mother.

In China the slave girl system had been a recognised institution for centuries. A slave girl was called a *mui tsai*, a Cantonese expression meaning "little younger sister". The word is sometimes used in a general sense, without reference to slaves, but it particularly refers to a girl transferred from her own family, either directly or through a third party, to another family to be used as a domestic servant. Such a girl was not given regular wages and was not at liberty to leave her employer's family of her own will or at the wish of her parents. A document was drawn up on red paper—as I witnessed in my own case—and the purchase money was handed over. The transfer was usually by purchase, but occasionally it was the settlement of a loan or a security for a loan. In the latter case, the girl returned to her parents when the loan had been paid back. By Chinese custom a *mui tsai* was not a slave in the Western sense, without any legal rights at all; she was a special type of domestic servant. The girl was provided with board and lodging, clothing and general care, and at a marriageable age she was given by her master to a suitable husband and presented with a dowry. However, in practice, these girls often became real slaves and were completely under the will of their masters. A number of reasons led to the development of this system. In China, girls had a much lower status than boys. Moreover, families were generally large and many lived on the verge of starvation. In times of famine, flood, epidemics or of disturbed political conditions, the situation became worse. There were few alternatives for the poor peasant. He had to choose between infanticide or letting the child be adopted or bought as a slave girl.

Infanticide, though practised, was naturally the last choice and the possibility of adoption, though preferable, was limited. An adopted daughter had a much higher status—the girl changed her name, was treated as a daughter, and was sometimes even given a little education. The middle course was to dispose of the child as a slave girl; this suited the employer. There was a demand for female domestic servants in well-to-do families and in this way the employer got a servant who would stay for many years and over whom he had far greater control than over a paid servant. So the *mui tsai* system developed.

In my own case the transfer was made indirectly through a trafficker in girls. Girls, were bought by the trafficker from destitute parents or from those who, for some reason, wished to get rid of a girl. The girls were then transported elsewhere, often overseas to Malaya, and sold at a profit. These traffickers also dealt in girls destined for brothels, but although some *mui tsai* did eventually become prostitutes the two uses of girls were distinct. In Singapore, at the time I arrived there, it was not illegal for a family to have a *mui tsai*, but if cruelty or ill-treatment was proven, the employer could be prosecuted; the girls involved in prostitution were dealt with separately under various ordinances for the protection of women and girls. Obviously, the *mui tsai* system was open to abuse and although many slave girls were treated well, everything depended on the character of the master.

My master was a rich man, a landowner, and he had many friends. He often had parties and got drunk, but fortunately when drunk he slept and was not violent. More often he suffered from insomnia, and then he would walk around the whole house visiting all the women's rooms. I had been told by the members of the household that he craved female company. After about three months he started trying to visit me at night. I cannot express my terror when I heard his footsteps. I crawled anywhere, inside cupboards, under the beds, outside the windows, anywhere, as long as I could get out of his reach. I never slept two nights running in the same place. Luckily for me the house was very large. Many a night I slept with my friends, the geese, but more oftten in a bathroom. One night when he could not find me. the old man complained to his wife who came with him to look for me. They searched the twenty-odd rooms, the garden and even looked into the well, then at last they found me under a platform on which stood pots of flowers. Neither of them could reach me so the woman took a long stick and struck me many times. I often wonder now how I stood that beating without making a sound. They even tried to force me out by pouring water over me. It must have been an hour after they had left me before I crawled out shivering with cold, my long hair wet. I dragged my aching body to the bathroom; I had never experienced such pain. It is very hard for me to describe the feelings I had then. It is very difficult for people to understand what it means to be a slave, to be bargained for and sold like merchandise, to suffer shame and the whips of one's master and mistress. But in sickness or in health a slave's work has to go on, so early next morning I was up to feed my chickens. While I was doing so our next-door neighbour looked over the wall. She was curious and wanted to know what had gone on during the night for she had heard the whipping and the shouting. She said, "If I were starving, I would not part with my children." The gossips began to talk among their friends, describing how my master and mistress treated their slaves.

Our household had many visitors, among them a Christian nurse. She was very different from the other visitors; she would go out of her way to talk to me, and gradually I was drawn towards her. One evening when she visited the house there was nobody at home and she took the opportunity of speaking to me. She said she was surprised to find me in this house, and that somehow or other she could not see me as a slave.

"Where are your parents? How did you come to be sold to this house?" she asked.

From that day onwards I called this charming Christian "Auntie". On another occasion while she was visiting the house, and we were out of sight of the old couple, she taught the other slave girl, my master's son and myself to pray. She told us stories of Christ's suffering and of His dying on the cross, and of Joseph who was sold as a slave. These stories were very comforting and real to me, but this reassurance did not last long. I prayed hard and even hung pictures of Jesus round my neck thinking that in this way He would protect me. I called to God whenever the old man came near me, but my troubles went on nonetheless.

Once a month the old man went to visit his estates in Johore and farther north, and I had to follow with the party. On these visits he behaved himself very well, for otherwise he would have lost face. One night, after returning from one of these trips, I was fast asleep in one of the empty rooms, when the old man found me. The fright I had on feeling someone touch me woke me up immediately and I shot out of the room like lightning, knocking the old man over. Within minutes the whole household, including the Bengali watchman, was searching for me. My mind was a blank, I could not think whether it would be better to jump into the well or to run away. Anyway I could not get beyond the gates so I climbed up a tree. I remained there for about two hours, and when everybody had gone back to bed I slipped down and went to sleep in a storeroom.

The next morning while I was cleaning the fish, the old man shouted at me, and the start I gave caused me to slice my finger deeply. The blood spurted out and I screamed, which put everybody into confusion. They all came to my aid, thinking I had injured myself seriously. After my hand had been bandaged up, my mistress felt sorry for me, and said she would take me to her aunt's house and that I could stay with her there in peace. I was overjoyed and left the same day.

We went by car and, after an hour's drive through many villages, arrived at a small village; through the window of the car I could see a neat little house standing near a fish pond. An old woman greeted us and took us into a hall where she worshipped her ancestors. My mistress was in a hurry and wasted no time in telling her that I was a very disobedient girl and that I constantly refused to go to bed with the old man, with the result that he was furious and blamed everybody. She herself did not know what to do, so she had brought me to her hoping that she, the aunt, would change me. Although I listened to the conversation I could not make out why the old man wanted to go to bed with me—not until the aunt explained to me later.

Ah Yee, which means aunt, was a very gentle woman with a soft voice. She showed me around the house which consisted of three bedrooms used by her two sons and herself. There was a well and near it a little hut where we took our baths. There were plenty of trees and vegetables and fruit, as well as ducks and chickens. I liked the family very much and I think they were fond of me too. I worked very hard; I cooked their breakfast, which consisted of rice pudding, salted eggs and salted vegetables, and I looked after the fowl. One morning Ah Yee told me that she wished I could remain with her so that I could marry one of her sons.

"You cannot remain a slave for ever," she said. "If you marry my son, you will be treated as an equal."

I was willing to marry her son, for only in this house was I allowed to sit at the same table with the family. I slept in a bed with Ah Yee and worked side by side with her. It was a long time since I had been treated so well. Yes, it seemed a very long time since the days when I had had the protection of my parents. I remembered the little parties I used to go to, the visits I paid to relations during Chinese New Year, the *ang pau* (red packets containing money) which I received, and the joy and happiness I had known. Now I seemed to have nothing. Chinese New Year was not very far off, but I hated it as it brought back the memory of the happy New Years I had spent at home. I told Ah Yee about the excitement of New Year celebrations in our village in China—how all the houses were opened to the public at that time. The brides who had married during that year were on show; they stayed in their houses dressed in their bridal gowns, and had to carry tiny trays with small teacups on them and stand in the centre of the hall for people to see them. Some came to admire, others to criticise. The admirers and the critics received, if they wished it, a cup of jasmine tea from the brides and when they had finished they returned with an *ang pau*.

Ah Yee told me that that was the Teochew custom but she thought it was no longer practised in Singapore. That city, she said, was too modern for her liking; she was shocked when she saw women in the company of men. Once she had seen a gathering in which men and women were locked in each other's arms. She said in tones of horror, "They call it dancing." Her marriage had been arranged and her married life happy, although her husband had died rather young. As she was speaking, I remembered a young man who lived next door to us in China, whose marriage had been arranged with a less satisfactory result. At the celebrations thousands of crackers were let off, and everybody wished him long life and many children. I thought the bride looked very beautiful, but the poor girl could hardly hold up her head because of the weight of her heavy jewelled crown. The next morning I heard yells in a most unintelligible language and saw the bride of the night before running away. The groom had been most unhappy and had lost face when he had discovered that his wife was deaf and dumb.

"This discussion on marriage," said Ah Yee, "reminds me that I must explain to you why your master bought you."

She explained that he had come to Singapore from South China. As the years went by, he made plenty of money but he wanted women. He had many, but he preferred very young ones. He had the peculiar idea that by having young girls he would be granted a longer life, and would remain young and healthy. As his present, second, wife wished to keep her position and to please him, she had suggested to him to import a few girls. As I said earlier, the terms which normally applied to a slave like myself were that if she were good and did her duty she should gain her freedom perhaps at the age of eighteen, and then be married to a man of her master's choice and be supplied by him with a dowry. Such a slave might or might not have become a concubine in the process. In my case it appeared that I was to be his concubine as well as his slave. I was horrified when I discovered what slavery was going to mean for me! Now I knew why the old man walked through the dead of night, visiting the women's rooms, dragging his two large slippers. A terrible sound it was to us all! Ah Yee told me that only the gods could help me. I looked at her with a mocking smile thinking, "The gods have too many people on their hands!"

A few days later my mistress came for me. I was wanted at home because Chinese New Year was approaching; the house had to be spring-cleaned, decorated and prepared for the multitude of friends and relations who would come to wish the family long life and a prosperous New Year. I was most unwilling to leave but I had no alternative. I was allowed to say farewell to Ah Yee's two sons. We did not shake hands; this custom was unknown to us, but we bowed. On the way home my mistress told me to be good. She added that her decision to buy me was the greatest mistake she had ever made in her life. The old man was in the house when I returned; he smiled and asked whether I had had a good time, and I thought it was most unusual for him to ask such a kind question.

From then on we were kept very busy preparing for the New Year. We were each given three yards of dress material to make something new for the coming year. We were told to observe the strict rules regarding the New Year, which lasted for fifteen days. After the house had been cleaned, we hung a piece of red cloth over the front door, and then erected a temporary altar in the garden facing it. This was for the worship of the god of heaven on the eve of the New Year. On the 24th day of the last month we worshipped the kitchen god; we had to please him as he left this earthly kingdom to report to the god of heaven. He reported on our conduct; whether we had been thrifty and kind, or whether we had used bad language during the past year; he also protected the household. The last day of the old year was the busiest, for we had to cook meals for the gods as well as for human consumption for the following day. I put on my new clothes and carefully combed my hair as we were not allowed to do this on New Year's Day. The house had also to be swept, for no sweeping was to be done the next day. It was considered bad luck to handle a broom on the first day of the New Year; wealth might be swept away.

A few minutes before midnight, two large red candles were lit and the worship of Ti Kong, the god of heaven, began. The master of the house bowed three times, followed by his wife. Then sharp at midnight thousands of crackers went off all over the neighbourhood to drive away the evil spirits and to welcome in the New Year. The mistress of the house suspected that our Christian friend was trying to put ideas about Christianity into our heads. She therefore ordered the three of us to be present. The master's son was very frightened of his father; to refuse to appear would mean a beating and no pocket money for the week. It was a great decision for us to make. We looked at each other, wondering if God would be very angry with us if we worshipped this god, but before we had made up our minds the mistress shouted at us to hurry up, as the servants were assembled to offer their thanks and to ask for long life. So we were rushed into it. We waited for more than an hour before we cleared away the table on which was placed the food for the gods. Some people believed that you had to wait until the joss-sticks had finished burning, while others thought an hour was long enough for the gods to eat. None of the household slept that night. The next morning was very busy too; innumerable relations and friends came and, as each visitor entered the house, he or she was served with a cold drink, sweets, cakes and red melon seeds, the child visitors receiving a red packet of money. The house was visited by a troupe of lion-dancers who danced and beat drums, and received large red packets of money. On the second day of the New Year the mistress went out visiting, since, on the third, everybody must stay at home because of a superstition that if you visited friends on this third day you were sure to quarrel with them during the year. On the fifteenth day of the first moon we were again busy, this time with the end of the New Year celebrations.

Unknown to me, changes were then taking place in Singapore which were to have a great effect on my life. For a number of years there had been public criticism, including criticism by the Colonial Office, of the *mui tsai* system, and the Chinese Protectorate knew of its abuses. In 1932, an ordinance (the Mui Tsai Ordinance) was passed by the Straits Settlement Government which aimed at controlling *mui tsai*. After 1 January 1933, no new *mui tsai* could be bought, all *mui tsai* had to be registered and it was forbidden to possess an unregistered *mui tsai*. Parts of the ordinance dealt with overwork or ill-treatment of *mui tsai* and the payment of wages to them. The powers of supervision and custody by the Protector were increased and penalties for failure to obey the law were heavy. By good fortune, 1933 was the year that concerned me, and all *mui tsai* had to register by 30 June (later extended to 30 September). I was one of 706 slave girls in Singapore who were registered during that year.

The other slave girl and I were told that we were going to a place to be registered; we were given new clothes and wore borrowed jewellery, and painted our faces in order to make a good impression. We went as adopted daughters. In the office there was a young European lady. She looked very beautiful to me, her skin was white and she had blue eyes; I thought she came from heaven. She held both my hands and spoke to me in Teochew (my own dialect). I could not take my eyes off her, and was spellbound by her gentleness. She told me she would visit our house at regular intervals and that we were to let her know if we were badly treated. She also told us to think of her as a mother. This conversation took place in private; our mistress was not present. On the way out this lady told our mistress that she would visit the house soon. On hearing this, our mistress was alarmed, and told us to dress nicely and to call her "ma" instead of Ah Neo—the difference between the address of an adopted daughter and that of a slave when talking to her mistress.

One day, the other slave and I held council. We decided that we had been slaves long enough, and that the only thing to do was to run away. I cut off my long hair without the permission of my mistress, who was furious with me. For some reason I thought my long hair would be a nuisance if I were to run away. We had no friends and we could not find our way farther than a few hundred yards from the gate, but we felt it was essential to get away from the house. I could not stand being beaten, eating the leftovers left me hungry, and I could not bear having to massage my mistress's fat body which I had to do every night. We thought the best time to disappear would be after dark when every member of the household was in the dining-hall, but to run away together would be fatal as we would be missed immediately. So the best plan seemed to be for my companion to leave the house while I served the evening meal, and if anyone asked for her I would tell them that she was gathering eggs in the garden which was one of her jobs.

The next day, to my great disappointment, I was told to look after a tiny baby whose mother had died soon after its birth. When the baby arrived I was surprised that they made so much fuss over a girl, for in China girls were considered useless and I recalled the many babies left on the road in the vague hope that someone might adopt them. It was not at all unusual to find a baby wrapped in a blanket and left on the roadside. The usual procedure was to unwrap the blanket, have a look at it and, if it were a boy, to claim him at once as an adopted son; but if it were a girl, a cent would be placed nearby and she would be left for the next passer-by to do the same. At times many cents surrounded a girl baby and I was told that sometimes greedy people would carry her home with the money, and then keep the money and throw the baby out. In the winter most of these babies died soon after they had been abandoned.

I remember my maternal grandfather hearing a baby crying outside the house one foggy evening. He insisted on going out to look at it, as he hoped to find a boy, having none of his own. When he returned we knew the answer from the sad look on his face. My mother was the eldest daughter and there were nine other girls, so when an eleventh one arrived she was most unwelcome. As Grandmother delivered all her own babies, and there were no witnesses, she strangled this one, and instructed Grandfather to bury her. A year later she gave birth to a boy who lived only a few hours and they thought that the baby girl's ghost had come to take its revenge.

In order to keep the family name, Grandfather adopted a son. When he was about fifteen years old this boy was suddenly taken ill. My grandparents believed the spirit of the dead baby girl spoke through him, and that she was very unhappy and was going to take her revenge on him too. The news terrified the family, who begged her to spare the boy. They said they would offer sacrifices to her. I remember that Grandmother took me to a paper shop and told me to choose anything I liked. (The girl would have been about my age if she had lived.) Later when I saw those lovely things being burned—the usual way of offering propitiation to spirits—I was very disappointed.

With all these thoughts in my mind, I smiled at the baby before me, and thought how lucky she was to be born in Singapore and to be loved.

That evening our welcome Christian visitor came. She was very disappointed when she saw that I had cut my hair and I then realised how foolish I had been. She was welcome not only to us, but to the whole family. That night everyone was busy entertaining her and we were left alone. I walked with my fellow slave to the gate; we pretended to look for eggs, as we had often done. The watchman was busy talking to a friend so she slipped out of the gate and I returned to my routine work, but my thoughts were with her. I was very jumpy and worried in case anyone should recognise her and bring her back. At about nine o'clock someone shouted for her; I stood stock-still until I was asked where she was. They searched the garden and every corner of the large building; the watchman was questioned and given notice to go. Everybody looked at our visitor as if she had something to do with it and I realised the mistake we had made—of course they would blame her because she was our friend. I would have given anything to have undone the deed but it was too late. She may well have noticed my guilty face for she took me aside and asked me if I knew the whereabouts of my friend, but even to her I lied. No one had much sleep that night, and there was even less for me, for I could not bear to think of the punishment we were going to get if she was caught.

Next morning I was up very early and had done most of the housework and was feeding the fowl when I saw the kind-faced European lady whom I had seen a few months before when I was registered. She came up to me and told me that my companion was with her. How she got there I couldn't imagine for I thought she had intended to go to a nearby police station. She took me by the hand and we entered the house to face the family. I was very ashamed, confused and frightened and I could not lift my head. The members of the family were equally embarrassed to find this European lady in the house so early in the day. She was the first to break the silence and at that moment I burst into tears. I was so confused that I cannot remember what happened next, but I followed the lady and we left the large house together—to freedom and to a life of my own, though I did not realise all this at the time.

I did not notice anything on the journey except that we walked up a very nice drive and entered a modern house, and I there found my friend seated in a comfortable chair. I was overjoyed to see her and wanted to know how she had got there. When she left the house it had been quite dark, and she had walked to a police station. There she told them who she was and they at once informed the Chinese Protectorate. Early the next morning she was handed over to an elderly European lady; my friend pointed her out to me, talking on the other side of the room. Her name was Mrs Winter. She was Lady Assistant Protector of Chinese, Singapore, at that time. She spoke little Chinese, but she was very kind indeed; I remember they gave us each a banana and told us not to be afraid but to tell her how we were treated by the family. She said she was going to take us to a very big home where there were many girls.

The Home was then called Poh Leung Kuk. It had been established in 1888, as a single room with six permanent juvenile residents. When I first saw the home it was on York Hill to which it had moved in 1928; by then it could take up to three hundred girls. During 1933 there were 423 admissions and 375 discharges, and between 200 and 300 girls were in the home at any one time. The iron gate was opened by an Indian and we walked up some steps. Mrs Winter spoke a few words to a young Chinese woman who was called Missie, then I turned round and was amazed to find a sea of faces. There were hundreds of girls all talking at the same time. Most were Chinese, a few were Indians, and, as I soon found out, they had all been slaves, orphans, singers or prostitutes. We lived in one compound in two buildings separated by a hedge. The first building housed two hundred girls, and in it there was a clinic, looked after by a Cantonese woman; a doctor came in when needed. During the day the girls stayed downstairs and did domestic work. Upstairs was a large dormitory where we were counted morning and night by a fat Chinese woman. The other building was much larger; it included a nursery and a big playground. There were two teachers, and I remember the cook, because she was very fat and had fishy-looking eyes—she looked as if she might eat you up, but later I found out that she was very kind.

It was a very strange life and I did not know then whether it was better to be in this large house or back where I had come from. I was given a pair of blue striped pyjamas and while I was changing a group of girls gathered around me in spite of my protests. They wanted to know why I had been arrested.

Someone shouted, "Are you an earning girl?"

Another one said, "Who is your boss?"

I could find no words but just stared at them. Some of these girls were about my own age; they could not understand the difference between slaves, orphans and prostitutes—neither could I. Most of them, however, were older. Suddenly a voice rang out calling for the two new girls.

The group beside me dispersed. Missie appeared and told us that Mrs Winter was going and wanted to say goodbye. I was in tears and wanted to go with her. Some of the girls burst out laughing, saying, "Who are you that a white woman should want to take you home?"

"You mustn't talk such rubbish," said Missie.

Then Mrs Winter said something in Cantonese, which confused me still more; I could not understand this language, which was the one generally used in the home.

Someone told me that dinner was at five and said that as soon as I heard the gong I had better hurry, otherwise there would be nothing left. "I always feel very hungry," she said. I was never hungry during the months that I stayed in this home—perhaps I was born a small eater, but I saw people who complained of hunger and of thirst, especially at night. We were shut up in our dormitory at six o'clock, and there were no taps which we could get at; so the bigger girls used to bully us and make us scrub the lavatory; then they forbade us to use it so that they could drink the water. Every ten minutes or so someone would pull the chain and then every drop of water was collected by the thirsty girls. At first the idea of drinking lavatory water shocked me but as the weeks went by I came to think nothing of it.

We worked in groups—some sewed, others cooked or went to school. At this time I was in the sewing class and here I made many friends. One friend I remember particularly. She was a singer, a very pretty girl, fair, with large black eyes and she had a very gentle and graceful manner. She had fallen in love with a taxi-driver of whom her parents disapproved. They used to meet in secret but were found out so they decided to elope together. They managed to get as far as a village a few miles out of Singapore but there the police caught them; the girl was only fifteen years old. I remember that she was very worried about what was happening to her boyfriend, for she had had no news from him for some months. She did not like the home, and said it was too noisy. Nor did I like it. Voices could be heard continuously and the chattering went on all the time. Quarrels were very frequent, but these did not usually last long and soon I would see the quarrellers walking hand in hand again. Unfortunately for me, my friend soon left the home. Her parents had asked for her and she was very happy because she thought she might now be allowed to marry.

After a few days I heard that our master and mistress were very angry with our Christian friend whom they blamed for our escape. They got hold of some of her clothes and shoes and laid them in the open outside the house, then, holding three burning joss-sticks they cursed her, accusing her of helping us to escape. Afterwards they tried to bribe us by sending us food so that we might be pleased and wish to return to their house, and so make people believe that they had treated us well. But we refused to have anything to do with them; they were no longer our master and mistress.

I had much time on my hands now, and missing family life I thought more of my parents than I had when I had been a slave, and I was very homesick. In the evenings when my sewing was done I would sit in the garden and picture myself back in China. Then I would be woken suddenly from my dreams by the sound of a gong; and it was time for bed. We filed in two by two and the usual counting of the girls began. Though I was homesick I was neither happy nor sad in this home. Principally I was deeply grateful to Mrs Winter and to her assistants who had helped me. But I longed to go out into the streets and see people—anybody—and I remember that, whenever Missie announced there was a load of firewood to be carried into the kitchen, I was the first to go for it. I fancied I could breathe more freely outside the iron gate but I do not know if others felt the same. All the same I liked being in the nursery and playing with the babies—children of some of the girls who had been brought into the home for protection.

One day we heard that Mrs Winter was ill; the news upset us all, and most of us wept. I often wonder if she knew how much the girls in the home loved her. She was so very kind, and those of us who had been ill-treated thought of her as someone more than human. As we two had been most recently admitted, most of the girls accused us of bringing bad luck.

"She brought you into the home, then she became ill," they said.

Later I learnt that she had been the saviour of many hundreds of girls like ourselves. Unfortunately, she died early in the following year, 1934. For many years afterwards her grave never lacked flowers. I for one visited it regularly until war broke out.

We waited anxiously for news of our future. Were we to be returned to the family? That thought frightened us. We longed to see our Christian friend who was so wise and sympathetic. I still carried the religious pictures which she had given me. The other girls laughed at me when they saw them and said, "Jesus is a European and He only helps white people."

"It is not true," I told them. "My father worshipped Him, though my mother did not."

Then one morning Missie called us to her office and told us that someone was coming to take us out somewhere. My angel-faced lady came and we were taken to a large building. We were asked many questions, such as "How many times were you beaten?" and "How much did the family pay for you?" There were endless questions. Then I was asked what I wanted to do—of course I wanted to go home to my mother. But I could not remember my address and no one could trace it. I was born in Hong Kong, but Hong Kong was a long way from my home village in China and no one recognised its name. Finally they decided that I should remain in the home and join the school there. After I had been in a Chinese class for a month, I was told I should now be sent to an English school. This did not appeal to me, even though I was told it would be good for me.

One bright evening a car came, and one other girl and I were taken to the school for a visit. We met three Europeans, Miss Heather, a white-haired lady who was sitting with her dog, Miss Kilgour and Miss Lane. Miss Lane, the Principal, had been a missionary in China for many years and could speak Chinese, but unfortunately I could not understand her, because she did not speak my dialect. The three of them stood up as we entered and Miss Kilgour said, "Good evening." I was anxious to reply. "Good..." came out but the "evening" would not come, it was so difficult to say. Miss Kilgour smiled and said something. Missie, who had brought us, continued the conversation and we were forgotten. Then it was time for us to return to the home.

A week later we were taken before a European and told officially that we were being sent to the English school. My previous master and mistress were very ashamed and offered money—whether under compulsion from the Chinese Protectorate or not I do not know—for our use. I got $700; my fellow slave was paid $500—perhaps I had had more beatings. Missie told us that we were not to tell anybody in the school where we had come from in case people should laugh at us. I was shocked to think that people could be so unkind as to laugh at our plight; later I realised it was wiser not to talk about our past. But now, for some time, I have thought differently and today I am not, as I used to be, ashamed of my history.

We went out shopping and everything I chose was made of green, blue and white striped material. Perhaps I had become so used to blue stripes in the Poh Leung Kuk Home that I could not appreciate other colours. During the next week we were busy preparing our outfits. All the material was made up into blouses and skirts. I am not quite clear whether this was done on an order from the school, but throughout my school days I wore nothing but skirts and blouses, even though most of the others wore Chinese costume. Each of us had a rattan case, two pairs of white rubber shoes and white stockings. I was very happy that I should be going to school, for my father had always wanted me to go even though there were very few girls in rural China attending school in those days. Indeed, I only remember one, who later chose her own husband and was the talk of the village.

We said goodbye to the girls at Poh Leung Kuk and were invited to return for a reunion dinner which they held at the New Year festival and celebrated every twelve months. We arrived at the Church of England Zenana Mission School in 1934, towards the beginning of the second term, and were received by the Matron who was a large elderly woman wearing Malay costume. She was an orphan too and had been brought up at this school. She spoke only Malay and English and no Chinese dialects. We left our luggage outside her dressing room and caught a glimpse of a dormitory which I thought not very different from the one we had just left. By sign language I understood that we were to make ourselves at home. My real school life had begun.

The Mission School
1934–1939

The Church of England Zenana Missionary Society (CEZMS) School is one of the oldest educational institutions for girls in the Far East. Its history goes back to 1842, when two European women were visiting Singapore, en route to China; while they were walking through the streets they saw mothers forced by poverty to sell their daughters. They got permission from the Governor to start a home for such children and placed it under the care of the London Missionary Society. So the school began, under a Mrs Dyer, in a house in North Bridge Road. In 1843 a Miss Grant came to Singapore as the representative of the Society for the Promoting of Female Education in the East, a society which had been formed in England in 1834. She took over the school and ran it until 1853 when Miss Sophia Cooke came to take charge of what was then called the Chinese Girls' School in which were about twenty girls. In the 1950s the school changed its premises several times. The main school building was finally built in 1861 in Sophia Road, where it remained until 1984 when it was demolished; the school relocated to neighbouring Wilkie Road in 1986 and is still there today. Miss Cooke was one of the most striking characters of the later decades of the nineteenth century in Singapore and was Principal from 1853 till her death in 1895. Soon afterwards (in 1900) the school passed under the control of the CEZMS and Miss Gage-Brown became Principal. For many years the school was the only one in Singapore giving elementary English education, together with religious instruction, to Chinese girls. From its earliest days it had also been an orphanage where many Chinese girls had been cared for.

I was chosen as one of two orphans for the year 1934. When I entered the school I discovered that there were a number of other orphans. I was very happy, and grateful to the people who had arranged my transfer to this school. I am even more grateful today. The CEZMS School not only gave me my education, but also a home, security, affection and personal guidance.

It was a strange and most bewildering sensation to be able to mix freely with people. I could hardly believe that I was a slave no longer. It was a comforting thought that I belonged somewhere. Early on the morning after my arrival, Miss Kilgour, a Scottish missionary, introduced me to a Chinese woman who was in charge of a "special class" for overage girls. It was held in a room separated from the main school building. I was happy to find that my teacher spoke my dialect. There were five of us in the class, two of whom were day girls. The special class was intended for girls of various standards of education, some almost up to the normal grades for their age, others like myself knowing no English. Because of its cosmopolitan population, education in Singapore has always been arranged on a linguistic basis: English, Chinese, Malay and Tamil schools according to the language used. Chinese, Malay and Indian pupils attended their own schools, but the English schools contained many races. The CEZMS School was an English school and so, for girls entering without a knowledge of English, it was essential to acquire this as rapidly as possible, since all future progress in the school depended on it. Without the coaching I received in the special class which concentrated on English I should never have understood the ordinary lessons.

At this time the school had about 300 pupils, most of whom were

Chinese. The classrooms, except for the one mentioned above, were on the ground floor of the main building. It was old and spacious with large rooms and very high ceilings. You entered it through a porch which led into an open hall with four classrooms opening off it, above which were the missionaries' quarters. The classrooms contained very little equipment, only desks, a table and chair for the teacher, a small cupboard where our books were kept and, of course, the inevitable blackboard. All the aids to learning nowadays used in a classroom were absent; there was, for instance, no illustrated material. Apart from the "readers" we used in our lessons, very few books were available. There was no library in the school during my first few years. The teachers were of various races. Apart from the missionary staff and a few English women, they were Asians—Chinese, Indians and Eurasians, who lived out and came daily to the school.

Our day started very early because no servants were employed except an old man who did the marketing. All the cleaning, polishing, cooking and even the care of the grounds was done by the girls. We were each allotted certain duties, and today I look back with mixed feelings on the two drains running down behind the main building which it was then my special duty to keep clean. In order to get our work done before the school started at eight o'clock, we began our day at five o'clock, about an hour before daylight. We were awakened by the Matron's alarm clock and we often wondered what would have happened if the clock had failed in its duty, but alas, it never did. Noisily we staggered out of our beds and were soon at our jobs.

My two drains gave no difficulty as I could scrub them in the evenings, and therefore I had only to sweep them in the mornings. When our tasks were done, we rushed to have our baths. We wore sarongs and bathed in an open space as there were no bathrooms available for the boarders. We shared a common changing room which was in front of a large iron tank filled with tap water, and it needed skill to be able to keep the sarong in place while soaping. This ability to wash and change under a sarong often proved useful to me later. It was the privilege of the old boarders to watch and laugh at the new arrivals. I remember one girl who, when trying to pour a bucket of water over herself dropped her sarong and, instead of picking it up quietly, screamed, thus drawing our attention to herself and then in her excitement fled away naked. Dressing was always done in haste, and the skirts, blouses, long white cotton stockings and rubber shoes were soon on.

By then we were hungry and it was a pleasure when it was already seven o'clock and time for a meal. With our tin plates and spoons we queued up in the kitchen where the senior students dished out rice and fish. We carried our food through the narrow kitchen door to the dining room which was opposite the main building and next to our special class. It contained four rather old tables and benches which creaked as one sat down or moved on them. The first-class boarders, who paid twenty dollars a month, sat with the Matron but there were very few of them. Except that they got an extra bowl of soup and did less housework, we were all treated alike. The free boarders, and those of us who paid fifteen dollars and under, occupied the three remaining tables. Grace was said before and after each meal. We washed our own plates and spoons and stored them in our changing room.

Our morning school began with "prayers": a hymn, a Bible reading, a talk either by the principal or a visitor, and a short prayer. Noisily we hastened to our classes and no sooner had we said "Good morning, teacher" than the school bell went and it was time for PT. We were detailed to our individual sections of the school compound. Our teacher usually gave us a broad smile, then shouted out, "Attention! Arms raise! Bend forward! Lower!" Someone would giggle and whisper, "Ha! I can see your knickers," or "Your stocking is dropping!" The usual punishment for giggling or whispering was to write a hundred lines: "I must not giggle." The majority of us did not like PT, perhaps because of our unsuitable clothes. It was very difficult to keep our stockings in place, because the elastic of the garters had perished by the time they had been used by previous boarders and then passed down to us.

After PT, lessons began. My favourite subjects were history, geography and English. My mathematics has always been hopeless. (When I said goodbye to one of my teachers on leaving school, she consoled me by saying, "No more algebra, and no more geometry." This, alas, was not true, because no sooner had I started nursing than I had to cope with percentage solutions and doses of drugs which were even worse. I always added a prayer for the patient's safety after calculating the dosage, even when I had consulted the dispenser!) Scripture was also one of my favourite subjects. It was rather important in a mission school and we had to learn a hundred verses by heart every year. This gave me time to think more about religion and before the year had ended I thought how wonderful it would be to be a Bible woman.

Fifteen minutes was the usual time for recess, when we collected our pocket money—two cents a day were given to small girls and sixty cents a month to the older students. It was a long time since I had been given money to buy sweets and I decided that I would put all mine aside, or save at least a cent a day. I remember that a few years later a schoolmate stole a twenty-cent piece of mine. I was very angry indeed and started a fight which resulted in both of us being called before the principal who, instead of punishing the thief, punished me! She said I had tempted her by leaving the money about. In my temper I shouted at her and said, "Since you encourage stealing, from now onwards I am going to be a thief"—quite a change from being a Bible woman! A few minutes later I was very sorry for having been so wicked. "God would surely send me to hell," I thought, so I took my punishment calmly—I was sent off to bed and given plain rice without any meat or vegetables.

School ended at one o'clock and after lunch those who were on cooking duty stayed in the kitchen; the others did their homework in a classroom next to our dormitory, under the supervision of the matron. The "cooks" were usually a senior student and a junior; only once was the mistake made of putting two of us small girls on duty. As it was still dark at 5 a.m. my classmate and I wandered off to the garden in search of paper for lighting the fire, but there we found a comfortable seat and went to sleep; before long the hungry boarders were upon us. The experiment was not repeated.

After four o'clock we were free and could do what we liked. I was always buried in my school books. I was afraid that if I failed I should be sent back to the Poh Leung Kuk Home, therefore I was not ashamed to ask for help from girls smaller than myself, even though the others laughed at me. We had dinner at five, followed by evening prayers. Only the senior students were allowed to stay up till 9 p.m.; the rest had to be in the dormitory by seven o'clock.

The dormitory was a long narrow room, very well ventilated. There were two facing rows of iron beds covered by planks and mats. Matron's bed was in the corner separated from us by a screen. As the lavatory was some yards away, she always kept her chamber-pot under her bed. A fish head could be claimed by those who emptied it next morning. An extra fish head was most welcome, therefore emptying the pot was no hardship. In fact as the days went by my friends and I looked forward to it, and it was a great disappointment when the pot was empty.

Soon after I arrived I was told that every Saturday we had to have a "stomach wash". It worried me a great deal to imagine how they were going to wash my stomach out; however, I was soon to know. Saturday was always the busiest day of the week; we had to clean the classrooms, dormitory, kitchen, the prayer hall and the twenty-four lavatories. Just before breakfast the school bell went and we all hurried to a little room below the principal's house. The matron and a senior student were in attendance; we were given a blue and white china bowl and as we walked past the matron we opened our mouths, showed our tongues, and according to the amount of fur on them we were given teaspoonfuls of salts. In no time the twenty-four lavatories were occupied. I managed to survive this for five years.

Sunday as a "Holy day" was strictly observed; besides cooking, which was compulsory, there was nothing much else to do. The Bible was the only book which we were allowed to read. It was considered wrong to look at one's lesson books or at story books, and we were not allowed to play games. The morning was partly filled by Sunday school. After lunch there was a compulsory siesta between one and four o'clock and then we had our final meal and dressed for church at five. We put on our best clothes including our long white cotton stockings. Whether it was raining or not, each one of us had to carry a paper umbrella. Then the crocodile of girls started off, with the principal or the matron walking majestically in front and the older girls forming the tail. We were taught a special way of walking: it was considered undignified to swing one's arms freely or to look to the right or the left. The church service was endured, and fortunately for us it was enlivened on occasion by the priest thumping the pulpit and startling the matron out of her slumber.

As I have said earlier, my father was a Christian, but in spite of this my religion was very mixed. All my relations on both my father's and mother's side were Buddhist, and, as far as I know, my father was the only Christian in the clan for generations. It is not to be wondered at, therefore, that although he was a prominent Christian in the village, my mother continued in the Buddhist faith. As a young child I naturally spent most of my time with my mother, so her religious practices had more influence on me than those of my father. My mother was very superstitious and consulted the gods in the temples whenever any family trouble arose and also insisted that all the necessary precautions against evil spirits should be carried out in our home. We did not, however, worship our ancestors at home—a practice that had no doubt been forbidden by my father. But he did not, or could not, prevent my mother going to the temples and this explains the many hours I had spent in them, especially when I was ill. It also explains the irrational fear of the gods which I retained throughout all my childhood, even though I put little trust in them.

I can recall one of my visits to the grave of my paternal grandfather. It was during a festival which takes place in the spring between March and April, and is called Ching Ming, meaning "pure and bright". Before we set out, I had been warned about the strict rules which I should have to observe, especially that I was not to touch anything before it had been offered to the spirits, otherwise the spirit might get angry, with the result that someone would fall sick. Grandfather's grave was on a hill, one among thousands in the form of a horseshoe. The graveyard was very bright with waving strips of coloured paper everywhere. We began our sacrifice by offering tea, cakes, pork, vegetables and rice and placed these at the foot of the grave. We knelt down in turn holding three joss-sticks, after which we burnt thousands of pieces of paper money. Then I was told to look after the offering while my relations moved on to pay their respects at other graves. I felt very hot and hungry and was tempted to steal the food. Eventually I decided I would do so, even if it should make my grandfather angry with me, so I began eating. When my relations found me doing this they were horrified and told me to ask my grandfather to forgive me, but I refused to do so. Two weeks later I said to my aunt, "Look, I am still alive."

On another occasion I visited Guan Yin—the goddess of mercy. Her temple was built on the top of a hill overlooking the sea, for she is the favourite goddess of seafaring folk and travellers. Women also worship her with great fervour. The temple was crowded with young women, most of whom offered powder and other toilet articles in the belief that the pretty donor would become more beautiful, and that even the ugly one would be made prettier. Like the others I burnt my joss-sticks and my paper money and left the temple to play with my friends. Then someone, seeing a bundle of unburnt papers near the altar, said to me, "You have not burnt your money yet."

"I have," I answered.

Of course she did not believe me and started an argument. It went on until someone suggested that we should consult Guan Yin, which we thought a good idea. So we did this. Returning to the temple I took the pair of wooden divining blocks. These were two pieces of wood shaped so that one side was convex and the other flat; they were commonly used to obtain the god's answers to a question. The blocks were tossed in the air and the way in which they landed on the ground was observed. If one faced upwards, and the other downwards, the answer was "Yes"; and this was the way they fell in my case, suggesting that Guan Yin believed that the unburnt papers were mine. I was furious, and pointing to Guan Yin I said, "You liar, I will never worship you again!" Incidents such as these, so vivid because they happened in my early childhood, left me with a feeling of doubt about the religion which had been taught me by my mother.

The Christian nurse I met as a slave had first introduced me to stories about Jesus and so, when I entered school, Christianity was not new to me. As the months went by, I began to think about the Christian religion. "Who is this God," I wondered, "and how can I find him?" My Sunday school teacher was very helpful, and it was owing to her that I was able to sort out what I believed. The Christians that I came most into contact with were the missionaries of the school, and I realised that if God could make the missionaries so kind and wise— especially Miss Kilgour—He must be kind and wise Himself.

Besides morning and evening prayers, we held a weekly prayer meeting at which we sang a hymn and each of us said a prayer in English or in some other language. This always led to giggling and laughter. But religion gradually meant more and more to me and during my second year at school I decided to be baptized. Miss Lane taught me in baptism class. I was very excited when I received my pretty new white dress; nine of us were baptized together by Reverend R.K.S. Adams on 11 August 1935. Miss Lane and Miss Kilgour were our witnesses. At my baptism I was given the name Janet and after that my Chinese name was less and less used and as Janet I became known to all my friends.

Time passed by very quickly so that before long I realised that the end of my first term at school had come. I had made many friends, both boarders and day girls. It was very sad indeed to say goodbye to them, and we all cried when we sang our end-of-term hymn:

Lord dismiss us with thy blessing,
Thanks for mercies past received;
Pardon all, their faults confessing;
Time that's lost may all retrieve:
May thy children
Ne'er again thy spirit grieve.

The boarders who had parents were busy preparing to go home while we orphans got ready our belongings for inspection. We were allowed a week in which to get our bits and pieces together and we spent a great deal of time ironing and mending. Then on the appointed morning we took our suitcases and all we possessed to the play hall which was in the main building and there we spread everything out on the floor. Miss Lane and Miss Kilgour began the inspection from the senior students downwards and each article was carefully examined, the torn clothing condemned, the suitable and usable ones passed from one to the other. A list of each student's clothes was kept by Miss Lane and when there was nothing she could find to fit a particular girl, new clothes had to be bought. Of course, we had no idea then how difficult it was for her to find money to buy our food and to clothe us, and we were not pleased when term after term we received old clothes. With sixty cents pocket money a month, it was rather difficult to save. I, for instance, was always tempted to buy sweets and ice-cream and yet there was soap and toilet articles and shoe polish to be bought. It was then that I learned to know the value of money—a lesson for which I have since been grateful. One of the boarders, a good friend of mine, was rather rich and she found washing and ironing very tiresome. I helped to clean her shoes and do her washing and ironing and in return she gave me one dollar a month, with which matron was able to buy a pretty new red Chinese suit for me. I wore it first to church but it was quickly noticed by the principal and involved me in much questioning.

We orphans did not like school holidays because then we were very lonely; most of the boarders went home and only a handful of us remained. We were not allowed out unless accompanied by the matron and then only on special occasions. It was always during school holidays that I thought of my parents most; perhaps it was when I saw the boarders go away with their parents that I felt most lost, unwanted and homeless. I remember that one such holiday fell on a Chinese New Year, and that the thoughts of all of us went back to those happy New Years which we had spent with our parents, but we pretended to be happy all the same. As usual during school vacations there was not much to do and Miss Lane, realising this, sent a few yards of calico for us to sew. Looking at the material, someone remarked, "This is used only for mourning." However, we cut it up and before beginning to sew I suggested that we should play a funeral game. We pretended that it was my father's funeral and we each tied a piece of the material round our heads as chief mourners and pretended to cry. As orphans we had all known some such tragedy in our homes so, of course, this brought sad memories back to us and from being a mere game it turned into a truly tragic scene when we all started wailing loudly. Miss Lane, hearing this, came to investigate. The scene must have touched her; girls were sobbing on the floor, some rested their heads on tables, others just stood. Even the matron, who accompanied Miss Lane, wept. The wise principal said nothing but gathered up the material and told the matron to take us for a walk. We felt terribly ashamed.

One evening we went to bed early and suddenly in the dead of night someone screamed. I knew that voice; the light switch was near my bed but my courage had gone. I covered myself with the blanket and sank deeper into bed. No one stirred in the room; the scream came again louder and more terrifying. Someone shouted, "Janet, switch on the light quickly!" When I heard my name, it seemed to give me courage. I switched on the light and everybody sat up in bed. The girl opposite me was sobbing and between her sobs she said, "There was a man in my bed." We were shocked and horrified. The missionaries must have heard the scream for they were soon with us. Miss Lane wore a long nightgown and her hair was loose; and then we were more interested in Miss Lane's appearance than in the man. She looked younger and even kinder like this. The police were informed and men were posted in every corner of the building but the intruder was not caught. We were unhappy and terrified, and dreaded the time when darkness would come. For a while we had peace but at examination time our visitor reappeared. My last subject for the day had been geography; I had said good night to Matron, and as soon as I got into bed I went to sleep. Suddenly I felt someone near me; thanks to the moonlight I could see the room clearly. I smiled to myself thinking it was only the matron who usually passed by my bed. The next moment I felt a hand, then instantly I was out of bed. All the girls screamed; it was an eerie scene, blankets and planks were all over the floor. The missionaries found the door broken in. More policemen arrived, but they never caught the man. It was after this that the whole dormitory section was wire-netted.

During the Christmas holidays we were always very busy decorating and spring-cleaning. Our usual Christmas presents were a cake of soap, a toothbrush and a face towel. As the years went by, we knew exactly what we were going to get, which took the interest out of the Christmas tree. But one Christmas I remember a very pretty Englishwoman came to the school and a few days later she took about six of us out shopping. We entered a very big toy shop and the beauty of the toys nearly took my breath away. We were told by this lady that we could choose anything we liked. I could not take my eyes off a very lovely doll which was priced at two dollars. When everybody else had chosen their presents, I still could not make up my mind. At last the kind lady, who I later learned was called Mrs Birch, asked if I would like the doll. I told her that never in my life had I possessed one and if I could have it I would treasure it always. Mrs Birch looked at me with kind eyes and said, "My dear child, you shall have the doll." I insisted that it cost too much, but she bought it. If Mrs Birch had only known how much we appreciated that trip to the toy shop I am sure she would have thought it had been worthwhile. For months we talked of nothing else but the kind Mrs Birch, and I treasured the doll beyond anything I had ever possessed. I kept it locked inside my suitcase and only took it out to have a look at it once a day.

During my first year in the special class I had three different teachers and many of my classmates also changed; at one time I remember there were only two of us in the class. By now I could understand a fair amount of English. It was a compulsory language in the boarding school and anyone caught speaking any other language had to pay a five-cent fine which was a great deal of money for us, and we were therefore very careful indeed.

Our activities outside school hours were limited. One of the teachers thought it was a good idea for me to join the Girl Guides because one evening she had found me loitering in the garden watching the Guides with interest. Some visitor gave me two yards of brown material for my uniform which matron helped me to cut out and sew. The Girl Guides were then holding an exhibition of handwork, and it was with mixed feelings that I found my uniform among the exhibits.

Sport was never my strong point. Tennis was a compulsory game which we played unwillingly. The good players naturally would not play with us. So we usually began a game of hide-and-seek. If caught we were not punished but warned that "God's children" would not do such a thing. Our excuse for missing tennis was always that we could not keep our long white stockings in place while concentrating on the game. Once a week the matron took us to a swimming pool which was only a few hundred yards from the school, but I never learnt to swim.

Before the end of my first year at school, we had a new matron, the old one having left for China. Our new matron spoke many Chinese dialects and she was also a good needle-woman. It was she who taught me dressmaking and embroidery and aroused in me a permanent interest in sewing and housework. I no longer looked after the drains but had two classrooms under my charge. It was my daily duty to dust these rooms, open the windows and sweep the floor. The scrubbing was left for Saturdays and then I had the help of other boarders.

The year after I entered school a new teacher, Miss Thackrah, arrived to help Miss Lane and Miss Kilgour. The school tended to stress training for home life for it was expected that most of the girls would get married after seven or eight years' education. From its earliest days the school had provided wives for Chinese converts and it was a normal procedure even in my school days for a man to come to the school to get a young wife. Miss Thackrah realised that this type of education was not sufficient and helped to modernise the school by training girls for wider service to the community, in business, nursing, teaching and other professions. She was a large woman and very kindhearted. I remember one Sunday evening before we set out for church, she sent us a basket of apples. Some of us began to cry, for we had never had any fruit except bananas. Someone said that she came from a rich family. But despite her kindness, somehow or other we were terrified of her. However, it was she who modernised the kitchens and made our domestic life much easier. We no longer used tin plates; these were replaced by pretty ones which were kept in the kitchen. Our dining room furniture also was changed and now we even had a real cook. We still continued our duties in the kitchen, but less often.

One of Miss Thackrah's greatest aversions was cats. There were always dozens of them miaowing in our compound and they seemed to get on her nerves especially at night. So she told us to catch the cats—a rather thankless task which resulted in scratches from the bushes and hedges as well as from the cats. The girls were not enthusiastic until she offered a reward of one dollar per cat. This large sum immediately aroused all our interest. At the faintest miaow all other activities were abandoned in our efforts to track it down.

Miss Lane, our principal, was rather short and fat. Before coming to the school she had been a missionary in China for many years. I was told that she had been brought up in a very old-fashioned home and that even at the age of seventeen she was not allowed to associate with the opposite sex. It was no wonder she treated us in strict Victorian fashion. Looking back now I often think how wise she must have been, for it cannot have been easy to teach and train so many orphans coming from so many different walks of life. But at that time we were young and we could not understand why Miss Lane punished us. We thought she was very severe but rumour said that her heart was on the wrong side of her body and that was why she didn't share our views. One afternoon I was allowed to go out for a short while with a senior student and I bought a pair of sunglasses and wore them on my way home. Unfortunately, as I entered the school gate Miss Lane happened to pass by and she noticed my unusual appearance.

"Where did you get these, dear?" she pointed to my glasses. "God has given you a pair of beautiful eyes. Why do you want to cover them? How much did you pay for them, dear?"

"Twenty cents," I told her.

She handed me twenty cents and took my sunglasses. I was furious and said to myself that when I left school I was going to wear sunglasses day and night.

Although I remember Miss Thackrah and Miss Lane vividly, it was the third missionary at the school, Miss Kilgour, who impressed me most. She had the gift of personal sympathy and understanding which she combined with stern discipline. Even when we girls were punished by her, we knew she loved us and it made us feel so ashamed of our wrongdoing that we did not do it again. We found out later the circumstances of her call to the mission field, and realised how typical it was of her thoughtfulness for others. It was on a cold wet night that a speaker from the CEZMS visited her home town in Essex. Thinking correctly that few would go out to the meeting on so wild a night she decided that she must go. Hearing of the need for teachers she there and then volunteered and came to Singapore to the school; that was in 1926. She was at the school during all my time there, and it was a joy for me to see her in England after the war just before she died.

For a while it seemed to me as though trouble and sickness always followed me. On one occasion I was sent to St Andrew's Mission Hospital with a minor illness. My friends said goodbye as they saw me go, since the idea of going to hospital meant death to us then. One friend told me, "Janet, be careful. In hospitals when the doctor cannot treat a patient he always gives an injection to kill."

In the hospital I met a Chinese woman; she was my first contact with the outside world since I had gone to the school and I spent many hours beside her bed. I was very lonely and during visiting hours I asked my friend for ten cents, and not knowing my purpose in asking she gave it to me. The next morning after the doctor's round I decided that I had had enough of hospital life and that I was going back to school. I managed to leave without being noticed. Once outside the hospital I could not find my way as I had never been out on my own before. I saw a bus coming and without knowing which way it was going I got in, and as we passed the cathedral, I thought I should ask God to guide me home. But after praying in the cathedral for about an hour I thought it was odd that I still could not find my way and once outside the church I began to wonder if God were really there. Soon afterward the matron, who had organised a search party, spotted me. She was angry that I had run away from the hospital and caused so much trouble, and in her anger she took me straight to Miss Lane. I was terrified and then realised that I had done wrong; when Matron rang the bell I began to cry. I was greatly relieved when Miss Lane, instead of being angry, asked me if I were hungry and offered me a piece of cake. This encouraged me to confess why and how I had run away from the hospital.

Before I had recovered from this illness I had another which made me miserable. I was told to read the book of Job; so I read the book of Job many times with comfort, but when the illness had lasted for months Job became meaningless to me. One day my friend said to me that I had leprosy because my skin looked dark after my illness. She meant it as a joke, but I was convinced it was true, so I retreated to my usual corner under the steps leading to the dormitory to cry my heart out. An older girl tried to comfort me by saying that the Reverend Adams, who was our regular visitor and of whom we were very fond, would visit the Leper Home, and they, the girls, would come to see me at regular intervals. When she heard of it Miss Lane was furious that God's children should start such a rumour.

A week later I was sent to the principal's office, and as I entered I noticed three women obviously waiting to interview someone. They realised that I was frightened and told me to take a seat facing them.

"Dear, when you were in hospital, did you make any friends?" asked Miss Lane.

I was unprepared for this and was very vague as to the friends that I had made, until suddenly it dawned on me that I had spent many hours with a Chinese woman. I could see the women were relieved when I mentioned her name—God's child had not sinned this time. To my great surprise I was then given a letter to read from the lady's husband. He thanked me for the many hours I had spent with his sick wife. I was dazzled that a man should write a letter to me and also confused when I was told to return the letter so that it might be kept in the office.

While we were at school, all our relations with the opposite sex were carefully guarded. In our homes too men and women observed strict rules about mixing with each other. Sex was considered an indecent subject which we never talked about. We were even very sensitive about articles of female clothing. In those days I would never have mended my underwear in the presence of another woman, for it would have been considered vulgar to do so. It was of course thought ugly and barbarous to show one's figure. Traditionally men were considered superior to women by their families and friends and we girls were told not to associate with them in any way. We were even told not to sit down on a seat recently vacated by a man since if we did so we might get a baby. Miss Lane, who had been brought up in a strict Victorian family and had lived many years in China, supported all these customs. We did not have any male friends, correspondents were chosen for us, and the only letters we received were from girls overseas who wrote once a year at Christmas. As the years went by we became very shy of men, and thought that they were either our superiors or else something evil. The term boyfriend was puzzling to us. Bibles and dictionaries were brought out, yet, after hours of searching, we were still in the dark as to the meaning of the phrase.

One year the school had a fun-fair to which many helpers came, most of whom were boys from our brother school—St Andrew's. This was the first time that we boarders had an occasion to meet boys of our own age. We were very shy and when spoken to could hardly reply. I heard one boy remark: "What do you expect from such a school!"

However, in the end I told one of them my name.

He asked me if I could write to him sometimes.

"Oh no! I am not allowed to write to any boys."

I thought I would have no occasion to meet my boyfriend again. But soon afterwards we were coming out of church one Sunday evening when I heard a shout: "Happy New Year to you, Janet!"

I recognised the voice, but held my breath; Miss Lane was in front of me and Matron was behind. His voice rang out once again: "Janet, Happy New Year."

Just loud enough to be heard I replied. When I looked in front of me I knew I was heading for trouble. As soon as we reached the school gate,

I was questioned as to who the boy was and where I had met him.

I had many friends, the closest of whom were Beng and Fong. The latter was a day girl. One morning Fong, who was then in standard four and about fourteen years of age, told me, "Janet, I won't be coming to school any more."

I was very upset that my best friend was leaving so I inquired what was happening to her.

"I am getting engaged to be married on Thursday, to a boy. It has been arranged by my parents."

"But Fong, what is the meaning of marriage?"

Fong did not know but said that her mother had told her that the boy was handsome and very nice. Later I learnt that many girls when they reached standard four or five, that was at the age of about twelve or thirteen, got married, and naturally these young mothers had no idea how to look after their families. Because of this the school eventually decided to begin mothercraft classes. We had lectures on infant feeding and the general care of babies, and for practical work we went to a nearby crèche once a week to bath the children.

It was not uncommon for people to come to the school looking for wives. I remember one day we were invited out for a picnic at the house of a Chinese family. We mixed freely with them but not one of us saw any men around. An ex-pupil, Ruth, who was temporarily boarding in the school, was with us. We did not realise that at this very time a man was selecting her as his wife from among us. One evening soon afterwards we were playing a beggar game. Ruth who was the beggar was going begging in a torn frock when she came face to face with an elderly woman. Of course she did not realise that this woman was her prospective mother-in-law. But the mother-in-law wasted no more time in the school and took to her heels. She had meant to talk terms with Miss Kilgour but not knowing where the principal's office was she had wandered in the direction of the boarding-house. Now the marriage was off, for it was considered very unlucky to meet one's future daughter-in-law begging.

I was in standard five when, on another occasion, a man came looking for a wife. This particular wife had to be a Hokkien and had to speak that dialect; but her education did not need to be higher than standard five. She must, however, be good at housework. Female beauty was not essential. The ones who came nearest to this prescription were Gek Eng who was then about sixteen and myself, then fourteen. An excuse was made for us to carry some books up to Miss Kilgour's office, and I suppose it was then that the man saw us and made his decision. A few days later I heard a rumour that I was to be married off soon. The childhood memory of my cousin's marriage brought tears to my eyes. I was so upset that I refused to eat or sleep and wept profusely. Miss Kilgour comforted me and assured me that she would not marry me off if I did not like it. In fact Gek Eng became the bride. The future husband gave a hundred and fifty dollars to prepare an outfit for her. They were allowed to walk in the school garden with the boarders dragging behind them. We were more excited than the poor bride—mostly because of the wedding feast. Matron and the boarders helped in the sewing and preparations for the wedding. The bride was neither happy nor sad; she did what she was told. We helped her to pack her dresses which were put in pairs and tied with a string of red cotton for good luck. On the third day after the wedding, following the Chinese custom, she visited us and long afterwards she still felt the school was her second home.

It may seem strange that a school should arrange the marriages of young girls like this, especially where European missionaries were in charge. The history of these marriages goes back to the early days of the school and was based on the traditional Chinese arranged-marriage system. When the early Christian converts were looking for wives, not many Christian girls were available, so they turned to the school where the girls had had the opportunity of receiving Christian teaching. A Chinese man, Mr Hoot Kiam, who married Yeo Choon Neo, one of the first pupils of the school, founded one of the oldest families of Straits Chinese Christians in Singapore. Women like her were scattered all over the East, including Malaya, Borneo and Foochow, and thus built up Christian families which became the basis of new congregations. The school continued this practice until the Japanese Occupation and it was one of the reasons for the emphasis on the teaching of household duties which was so characteristic of the early education given in the school.

Though very little pre-marital advice was given, because of traditional reticence, most of these marriages seemed successful as the suitors were carefully chosen. Each had to be a Christian, to promise that he would have only one wife, and his family background, health and character were investigated. This generally meant that the man was of a suitable type and would treat his wife well. The new wife in those days had little sense of independence as she was, and expected to be, a comparatively unimportant member of the husband's household. Her duties were to serve her husband under the control of the mother-in-law and to raise a family. She accepted this status as a natural thing. In Singapore the vast majority of marriages were arranged by the families concerned. When I was in the Poh Leung Kuk Home I saw two marriages of this sort which were supervised by the Chinese Protectorate. The men visited the home, no doubt after careful investigation. The girls who were on the marriage list were previously notified. It was very funny when they asked one another in the dormitory, "Do you want to get married?" and went on to encourage each other as though it was some everyday happening. Later, these girls were lined up and walked one by one past the office and the man pointed to the girl he wanted. She had to accept or refuse on the spot. Usually it was considered worth getting married in order to get out of the home. The man had to provide some money for the girl's trousseau which we helped to prepare, and then on a lucky day according to the horoscope the girl was married. The bridegroom, dressed in his best, arrived at the home and went to the matron's office. The girl was then produced and the couple walked together down the steps towards the open gates while we lined the way and cheered.

As time passed, many of the old-fashioned ways of the school changed. A year before I left, Miss Inge, a missionary from England, came out and helped to modernise the school. Her coming altered the lives of the boarders. She paid us regular visits and mixed with us freely. Gone were our long white stockings; we began playing basketball, which we liked and for which we even wore modest divided skirts. It was decided that girls who were leaving school soon should be allowed to go out and to join clubs. With another Chinese girl I joined the Church's Young People's Club whose members were mostly St Andrew's boys and CEZMS School day girls. I felt very shy with the boys. Every time I was spoken to, I blushed and could not find words in which to answer. One visit to this club was enough for me, but Miss Kilgour told me that I must mix more with people as I should soon be earning my living.

I was in standard five, at the age of fourteen, when I was allowed for the first time in my life to go to a cinema. It was an educational film called Marco Polo. The thrill I felt, the wonder of the large picture-hall and the beautiful curtain nearly took my breath away. I sat with my classmates, most of whom had been to this hall many times before, so that to them it was quite ordinary, but to me it seemed something beyond my understanding. When the picture started it was so real to me that I forgot I was in the midst of so many people. There was a scene in which the hero fought a leopard, and realising to my horror that he might be eaten up at any minute I knelt down to pray, to ask God to protect him. Suddenly I was brought back to earth by hearing someone laughing and saying, "Look at that fool, where does she think she is?" I was so ashamed that for the rest of the show I repeated over and over again, "It's only a film!"

When I was just under sixteen I was told that after the age of fourteen girls should start to think about their future careers. I wanted to be a salesgirl because they looked so smart and painted up, but Miss Kilgour convinced me that nursing was a better life for girls. A choice of career was forced upon me by a change of the status of the school. In 1939 it received a Government grant-in-aid, and the overage girls had to leave. As I had started my education so late, I was one of them. It was decided that I should join the St Andrew's Mission Hospital as a nurse-in-training. But by the end of 1939 I was still only sixteen and a half years of age, and when I saw the matron of the hospital, I was told that I was too young to work—too old to study and too young to work! What was I to do? I had passed standard seven, and had spent about five and a half years in school. Looking back now, I wish I had had another five years. Education is not everything, for without practical ability and personal character and some ambition even a person with a good education does not get very far. But education is one of the most important foundations, without which all one's work and career are made more difficult. When girls came to me in my position as Matron of St Andrew's Mission Hospital, to ask about nursing, I always advised them to continue at school for as long as they possibly could before they actually started nursing. It was later in 1939 that I was told that the hospital had after all a vacancy for me. I heard this with some concern since for five years now I had had the shelter of the school, personal guidance from the missionaries and the companionship of the boarders.

The school had become my home with all that that meant to me; the insecurity I had previously known gave me a deep sense of uneasiness. Moreover, I knew that whereas most nurses could go back to their own homes when off duty, I could not go back to the school in this way. All this emphasised my lack of a real home and of the loving care of parents. Once more I felt alone in the world. But not quite alone: Miss Kilgour was full of thoughtfulness for me. She said, "Janet, be ready by ten o'clock and I'll go down to the hospital with you."

A rattan suitcase was all I possessed. The boarders had asked their teachers' permission to see me off. They formed a line at the main entrance to the school building. Goodbyes were said very quickly as we tried to blink away our tears. As I walked down the drive my schoolmates called out, "Come back and visit us." Soon I was at the hospital where an old Chinese man opened the grille and I was ushered towards the lift. Miss Kilgour helped me with my luggage to my bedroom and then left. I felt lost but I had no time to think about my feelings. The matron called me.

"You are to go on duty this afternoon," she said.

The Mission Hospital
1940–1941

I began duty at two o'clock. Dressed in my white uniform I thought I could not move freely. But I had not had time to take in my surroundings when I was asked to help move a body to the mortuary. I was terrified. The woman was dressed and covered with a mortuary sheet and I was told to stand on the top of the bed so that I could lift up the body on to the trolley. I had no time to think but struggled with the very heavy weight. At last three of us succeeded in placing the body on the trolley and pushed it towards the lift. The mortuary was opened by an old man who smiled, which I thought was very rude, as one should pay great respect to the dead. It was a very gloomy place, dark and smelly. We went through one door, then another and yet another.

"Why so many doors? Are you trying to shut in the ghost?" I asked the senior nurse, who glared at me and said, "Don't be bold!"

I walked slowly back to the ward thinking of the body that I had left behind. It was 3.15 p.m. and I was told to go for tea.

But then someone shouted, "New nurse, you are wanted in the delivery room."

"What is a delivery room, and where can I find it?" I asked.

I saw a woman groaning in great pain and I stood near her helplessly. The staff nurse told me to lift up one of her legs and at the same time she removed the blanket which covered the lower part of her body. I was shocked and very embarrassed indeed.

"I hate nursing, it is undignified and crude," I thought as I ran towards the door, but I was pulled back and the woman's leg was pushed at me again. "Goodness, what is coming—something black?" I shouted.

"It's the baby's head advancing," I was told. The leg was getting heavier and heavier and my knees were shaking. I whispered to the servant beside me, "I am going to faint." She took over and for a few minutes I sat on the floor to recover. When I got up the baby was on the table and the mother had stopped shouting. The nurse was attending to them.

"What is she doing? Pulling intestines out of the poor mother's stomach? God, please send me back to the school; I cannot stand this any longer," I prayed.

At last to my great relief I was allowed to leave the labour ward. Soon it was time for dinner and we crowded into the small dining room. I could not eat, but felt a lump in my throat. "If only I could talk to someone," but alas, there was no one to talk to me. I came off duty at ten o'clock, had my bath and got into bed but I could not sleep for thinking of the woman and the birth of the baby. I had never been properly told how we came into the world. It was 1 a.m. but still I sat near the window and thought about the day, about this first day as a nurse. The staff nurse who had been in the labour ward came past my room as she was on call. Seeing me up she walked in.

"Janet, not asleep yet?"

I had known her in school, so I was able to question her. "I never knew you were so cruel, pulling that woman's intestines out; how could you do such a thing after all the teaching you had at school?"

"You silly girl, that was not the intestine. It was only the baby's cord!"

Such was my first introduction to St Andrew's Mission Hospital.

When I went to the hospital, the Medical Mission had been

functioning for over twenty years. In 1913 it had begun as a small clinic in a shop-house in the Chinatown area of the city but by 1923 the work had grown so much that it was necessary to build a hospital. It was a three-storied building which stood in the most congested area of Singapore where the population density in some places exceeded 1000 people to the acre. Near to the building was one of the main markets which made the hospital noisy, especially in the early morning. On the opposite side of the building were rows of tenements where we could see and hear mahjong being played day and night, interspersed with domestic quarrels. The main wards, except for a children's ward, were on the first floor of the building, so were the delivery room and the operating theatre. The staff and nurses were housed on the second floor, and the chapel was on the same story. The best part of the building was the flat roof where the tubercular children were given a sun-bath every morning and where the staff could also relax when off duty. The building was a curious shape, rather like a diamond; down its centre was an airwell which provided a bird's-eye view of the activities below.

The Outpatients Department, which consisted of a consultation room with a small section partitioned off for examinations, was on the ground floor. Also there, was a waiting room and a dressing room, and between these two a dispensary, looked after by two Chinese men. The waiting room was small but here were rows upon rows of benches which were occupied by women and children of all faces and creeds who came from the nearby slums. As the hospital stood in the most densely populated area of Singapore, the poorest patients came to us and received treatment virtually free of charge. In this busy section the interpreter gave out numbers daily, so that the patients could see the doctor in order. In the midst of this chaos of shrieking children, the babble of different languages and the interpreter shouting out patients' numbers, stood a Bible woman endeavouring to save souls, but the patients were more anxious to be seen by the doctors than to be saved. In the dressing room there was a nurse who was in constant attendance doing dressings, giving general advice and seeing to the patients' needs. Some of these patients were very grateful and, poor as they were, they brought gifts to the nurses. Generally they could not afford more than a few bananas. These gifts were more appreciated than gold. These patients were very unlike some of the educated people who occasionally came to the hospital and who often demanded to be seen first. If the nurse were bold enough to say, "Please wait your turn," she was heading for trouble. I am sorry to say that some of the Christians also behaved in this manner.

One day a woman said to me, "Nurse, let this patient be seen first because she belongs to our church."

"What difference does that make?" I asked.

"You are a rude and bold nurse," I was told.

This sort of thing was a frequent occurrence and ever since then I have felt strongly—a view, I am glad to say, shared by the post-war staff of St Andrew's Hospital—that Christians should not have priority in treatment, but that they should be treated like everyone else. Indeed it seems to me that the Christians so far from demanding extra privileges should be willing to be like Jesus, in this case to wait longer, for "it is more blessed to give than to receive."

Work in the wards was less hectic and noisy than in the Outpatients Department, but like most nurses, I disliked night duty. As a "runner" I had to be everywhere: Children's Ward, General Ward, Outpatients Department and carrying legs in the Labour Ward.

"Janet, come here." I ran up the steps and stood out of breath in front of my senior nurse.

"Make me a cup of coffee."

Before the cup of coffee was ready I was wanted in the Labour

Ward, so it was either coffee, changing baby napkins or carrying "legs" through most of my nights on duty. I soon became used to removing bodies to the mortuary, but I still dreaded the delivery room. So many of the patients were violent, pulling their hair and screaming with the pain. It seemed to me that more babies arrived during the night than the day. On the arrival of each baby, the nurse, as a matter of routine, showed it immediately to the mother for her to establish the sex. There were always smiles if it was a boy and curses when a baby girl was seen.

Although a junior probationer, I had sometimes to look after very serious cases. Once I was nursing a woman with tuberculosis who was very wasted indeed. Her big eyes stared and her breathing was getting difficult; I was told that she was dying and that I had to feel her pulse continuously. The tiny ward was dark and too quiet for my liking. Stories I had heard suggested that hospitals housed a host of ghosts especially in dark corners. Tensely I watched the corners, one hand on the patient's pulse, legs wide apart ready to bolt instantly. As the shaded light swung with the breeze it cast monstrous shadows on the wall. They seemed to move about as though millions of evil spirits were waiting for this poor woman and perhaps for me too. For once I wished that someone would call me to the Labour Ward. My fear increased so much that the slightest noise, even that of the house lizard calling "Cheep, cheep", was enough to make me bolt out of the ward. One such rapid exit caused a disturbance because I ran into and almost knocked over the Medical Officer-in-Charge, who rebuked me severely, particularly as I could not give a sensible explanation of my unusual behaviour.

I remember one woman well because she was unusually pretty. She was in great pain and had asked me to rub her chest. Later she confided to me that she was the first wife but her husband had two others. Her baby girl, who was only a few days old, was still in the hospital and she feared her husband might sell the girl when she died. I was asked to tell him from her, "You are not to sell any of my children, but buy me a good coffin and dress me in seven layers of clothing and worship me regularly." She thanked me and wished me a better husband than she had. I could not understand why her husband should want another wife when his first one was so pretty and young.

The nurses' quarters were on the top floor of the building. The rooms, housing three or four nurses each, were rather small and barely furnished: beds, a chest of drawers, a writing-table and one or two chairs. I used to long for a dressing-table. I was in a four-bed room; the room opposite was the dining, sitting and lecture room in one. It had two dining tables, two settees, a cupboard in which lecture materials were kept and a blackboard.

We worked by shifts from 6 a.m. to 2 p.m., 2 p.m. to 10 p.m., and 10 p.m. to the next morning. Our night-shifts lasted a fortnight and on coming off duty at 6 a.m. the same nurses had to go on again at 2 p.m. There were no nights off such as other hospitals had. Indeed there was not a single day off from one year's end to another. As a result the nurses started comparing their conditions with those of nurses in other hospitals and discontent grew. We had to keep strict rules about late nights—we had one late night a week when we were allowed out until 10 p.m. Ordinarily every nurse had to be in the building by 6.45 p.m. and the nurses who came off duty at 2 p.m. could not go out until 4 p.m. as they were obliged to take a compulsory siesta. The afternoon nurses although nominally free in the morning were made to clean the chapel at 10 a.m. exactly, neither sooner nor later—why, I could not understand.

Nurses who behaved like good girls and followed these rules had a hard lot if they had boyfriends. One night I was invited out by one of the senior nurses. She wanted me to meet her brother. I was thrilled. It was 8.30 p.m. when we left our quarters, a time at which we should have been in bed. When the boy arrived I lost my voice and felt shy and uneasy, for all the time I was thinking: "How are we going to get back into the hospital? The main gate will be shut." But my friend reassured me, saying she would bring me back safely. It was 10.30 p.m. when we arrived at the hospital. We tiptoed round the back yard to a small door next to the mortuary. But the small door was shut. We knocked and called out softly, "Ee Pak, *tolong* [help]." There was silence. I was scared because the thought of spending the night out of doors terrified me. Then all of a sudden the watchman's voice rang out, "You naughty girls out again!"

"Sh! Sh! *T-o-l-o-n-g*, Ee Pak."

Ee Pak stood outside the mortuary door holding a broom and feeling rather important. He eyed us critically and said, "You young girls think of nothing but boys; I have never taken a girl out yet," and he thumped his chest.

"*Tolong*," we pleaded once again.

"Come in quickly before the matron catches you or my salary will be cut." Perhaps Ee Pak had been told by the matron not to let any nurses in when they came back late. Thankfully we scrambled up the steps to our rooms.

Ee Pak had come from China as a rickshaw puller. He was an opium addict and completely destitute; he had no shelter and did not know where his next meal would come from. The hospital took him into service as a watchman as well as odd-job man and he served it faithfully for twenty-five years. As far as I know he never married; opium was more important to him than a wife.

"Ee Pak, so-and-so will make you a good wife," we used to tell him.

"Ha, women are not in my line, give me opium every time." He held his thumb up. Be Pak's salary was twenty dollars a month—just double my pay. Our salary began at ten dollars a month with two dollars fifty cents increment yearly. This was just about half the salary received by nurses-in-training in the Government Hospital. When in 1941 the war broke out Miss Kilgour asked me how much I had saved. She was horrified when I told her that I had not saved anything; all I had was a ring which I had bought for five dollars. In school, I had received only sixty cents a month, but everything was provided. Now that I was earning my living, I had to buy stockings, shoes and clothes; and my outings cost a certain amount.

Even after I had been a nurse for about eight months I was still unsettled, as in the hospital there was no home-like atmosphere. I visited the school almost weekly—it was the only home I knew. The days I spent with the boarders were the happiest, for I felt proud to be able to tell them stories of the outside world. Many times I was urged by friends to give up nursing, but although I was tempted to do so, I wanted to complete my training so that I could afford to go back to China and look for my mother, of whom I had not yet stopped thinking. I always hoped that every new patient who came into the hospital might perhaps be my mother. I felt sorry for the very old people and always thought of them as though they were my own mother or grandfather. I could not bear to see them doing heavy work, and for this reason I once ran across the road and tried to help an old man with a heavy load of firewood.

My roommates were very popular with boyfriends and they often exchanged letters making appointments—we were not allowed to use the telephone. One of them, Mary, an attractive Chinese girl, one year my senior, was my adviser and helper throughout the years we were together, and she is still one of my closest friends. She would go out and buy material for me which she would make up during her free evenings. Whenever she was invited out by her friends she would insist on taking me with her. I suspected that her friends were not always very pleased with my company, for I once overheard a conversation in which it was said that I was too shy, too old-fashioned, and besides this that I was an "elephant" weighing 130 pounds!

My free evenings were spent mostly at the movies, which fascinated me; I also took up dancing—a recreation which would have shocked my parents. Some days I felt terribly lonely and homeless, especially when my nurse friends called out, "Bye-bye, Janet, I am going home."

"Oh God, why did you make some people so lucky and others not? Please take away my lonely heart," I often prayed.

It was in my second year of nursing that I made the acquaintance of Dorothy who was a nurse at the Singapore General Hospital and it was she who introduced me to a family by the name of Chan who had three sons and no daughters. This combination was considered unlucky for the following reason. A Chinese written character meaning "boy" when combined with a group of strokes forming the character meaning "girl" makes a new character meaning "good"—the inference being that you cannot have good fortune unless you have both boys and girls. Mrs Chan was therefore anxious to adopt a girl into the family, and in their kindness they gave me a home. They gave a small feast to welcome me and even today they still think of me as a member of their family, and I always refer to Mrs Chan as my adopted mother, although, of course, it was not an adoption in the legal sense involving a change of name. I often went to their house when I was free, and so now, when my friends left the hospital saying, "I am off home," I no longer had that sense of loneliness, that feeling of not being wanted, for I too could say, "I am going home."

It was the lack of homeliness in the hospital that I noticed most. Compared with present conditions, of course, those which we worked under were very poor, but at that time this did not strike us as forcibly as it would today. The thing that did strike us was the lack of personal contact with the senior staff. We were not bullied or ill-treated by our foreign missionary sisters or doctors. Indeed, all in their own way tried to help us, but somehow we felt a lack of understanding and sympathy, a failure to enter into our lives and to identify themselves with our ideas and with our feelings.

One morning I was told that Sister X wanted to see me; her very name gave me the shivers.

"Nurse, will you tell your friends not to phone you!" she said sternly.

I did not know where the call had come from, nor was I told, but I apologised. There were two telephones in the building—one in the matron's office, the other in the sisters' quarters, but we nurses were not allowed to use either of them. A week later I met my friend who said to me, "My goodness, what sort of sisters have you got in your hospital? I telephoned to tell you that my mother had died but instead of taking the message, the person who answered gave me a scolding."

We put up with having no telephone but we did hope and even pray that we might sometimes be allowed to use the lift. When any injections or drugs had to be checked by the sister or doctors we had to climb the endless steps to the roof where the European sisters and doctors were sipping cups of tea. One day when we came back from church the doctor went up in the lift, and left us to climb the steps although we lived on the same floor. "Why this difference?" we used to ask.

On another occasion I overheard a foreign missionary scolding a nurse, "You dirty stupid Chinese, you are so unlike the Japanese who are very nice people, so my father tells me. You Chinese are stupid, now get out."

We junior nurses took council; to be scolded for our work might be justified, but that our nation should be condemned was not to be borne.

One of the girls said, "What have my father and forefathers done to her that she should condemn us?"

To report the matter to the matron would, we thought, be useless as one of the nurses said, "Blood is thicker than water." However, we prayed that the Japanese would come to Singapore soon so that our "dear" sister should be in good hands. Later she was asked to leave the hospital, and by a stroke of tragic irony, her ship was bombed by the Japanese and she was drowned.

This was typical of some of the missionaries—why they were ever sent to the mission field when they had no interest in the local population always surprised me. However, in 1940 a new sister, Miss Muriel Clark, arrived. She was graceful as well as gentle. We called her the pretty sister. Life began to change a little when she took an interest in us. She helped us in our ward work and taught us to prepare various trolleys and trays. She often visited us in our rooms. Once I was sick and she sat by my bed and nursed me, a kindness I still remember. We loved her. Once we asked, "Dear sister, why don't you get married, you are so pretty?"

"Go on with you," she said, with a smile.

She was our friend and we could confide in her if things went wrong in the wards. For instance, we had an elderly woman suffering from tuberculosis, a disease which needs long hospitalisation. She was baptized in the hospital and thought that as a result she was due to be enthroned—we called her the duchess and she lived up to her name. She did not feel that she should be treated in the same way as other patients, because she had become a Christian and was therefore superior to others. The duchess gave the nurses endless trouble. I myself was twice summoned to the matron's office because the duchess had complained that my service was not prompt enough for her liking. She was well enough to go out for the whole day, but once back in hospital she wanted to be waited upon. One evening we were very busy when she demanded a bedpan. Sister answered for us, "You can go to the toilet yourself."

"I don't want to."

"If you don't want to, we cannot help you," said our pretty sister.

"I will do it in my bed."

None of us thought that she would carry out her threat, but she did. Sister knew that we were afraid of further summons from the senior staff, and reassured us that she would take full responsibility and would explain the incident to the doctor.

It was about this time, during my second year, partly as a result of some of these experiences, that I felt uncertain about my religion. Perhaps I had believed that all missionaries were like Miss Kilgour, who was so kind and gentle and, above all, so full of understanding. Today I realise the good fortune I had in being brought into contact in my school with an outstanding group of missionaries—Miss Kilgour was undoubtedly one of the greatest woman missionaries in Singapore in my generation. Moreover, the Church of England Zenana Mission taught me a particular type of Christianity. The CEZM as a missionary society has always tended to be Low Church, stressing personal salvation and the quality of one's personal life. We usually went to church once a week but we were taught at school that church-going alone did not make a good Christian of one. Miss Lane once told me that Jesus would be pleased to see our work done well and that we should show a good example to our fellow men rather than only sit still and pray.

"The good work in you shines out," she said.

I am grateful for having been brought up in this way; the Chinese have always attached great importance to personal relationships and this religious teaching fits in with our way of thinking. At school we had prayers twice a day. The morning service in the assembly hall was conducted by the principal and attended both by the day girls and the boarders. The evening prayers, taken by Matron or a senior student, were very short and simple—a hymn and a prayer only. It was informal and gave us a sense of freedom of worship; perhaps this was owing to the fact that we were young and took it as part of our school life. When I went to the hospital my experiences with the chapel services were not entirely happy. Here the services were compulsory. Morning prayer was celebrated at 7 a.m., conducted either by the doctors or sisters, and every nurse, even those on duty, had to attend. We sang a hymn, the Scriptures were read, and there was a short talk followed by prayers, the whole service lasting about half an hour. At 10 a.m. prayers were taken in the ward by a member of the senior staff or by a Bible woman. A hymn was sung in English and if the Bible woman was conducting the service, the rest of the talk and of the prayers was in Cantonese—which because of the multitude of Chinese dialects was almost as unintelligible to many patients as English. If the service was taken by the doctor or by the sisters, then it was conducted in English, the Bible woman acting as an interpreter. These prayers were attended by the senior staff and by all nurses on duty. We knelt on the cement floor and the patients sat on their beds. Some patients looked on this daily event as a joke, others watched it with an interest which led to a few baptisms every year. Evening prayers were at 6.45 p.m. and were conducted in the same manner as the morning service. Because it was a compulsory service and held at such an odd time, we attended it with resentment—if there had been no chapel service, perhaps we might have been allowed out for a little longer. After a compulsory siesta from 2 to 4 p.m. we had tea, and the time from tea till chapel at 6.45 p.m. was too short for shopping and general outings. We felt that we were no longer school children but women earning our own living and we would have liked a little more freedom. When I was caught hiding during chapel I told one of the sisters, "Religion is something which must grow naturally in a person and cannot be forced."

I also told my friend Mary, "There are so many prayers, I find it difficult to know what to say to God."

"Perhaps God is getting tired of hearing your voice," she answered.

Holy Communion services were celebrated once a week by one of the priests of the parish. This service was attended by the nurses dressed in full uniform and was accompanied by what seemed to me an unnecessary amount of ceremony. Even though our chapel was a small room barely big enough to hold all the nurses at one time, the priest was always dressed in elaborate vestments, a server was in attendance, and occasionally incense made the fanless room even more stuffy. The lack of friendly contact with the senior Christian staff and this over-emphasis on attendance in chapel, have left me with a deep distrust of the kind of church-going and devotional exercises which do not result in Christian behaviour.

Looking back at the pre-war hospital, especially after having myself had some administrative experience in the post-war hospital, I can now see the difficulties under which it was working. During my years of training it had reached its lowest ebb. The hospital had put all its effort and thought into building and starting a new hospital for children with tuberculosis of the bones and joints (St Andrew's Orthopaedic Hospital, which was opened in 1939). Dr Patricia Elliott, the senior doctor of the mission, had become Medical Officer-in-Charge of this hospital and so the great influence she had exercised since 1926 at the St Andrew's Mission Hospital was weakened. There were many changes in the hospital's senior staff and, as I have indicated, not all of them were suited to the work. Yet, despite this, the hospital helped me in two ways.

Firstly, by the type of training that I received. There were very few teaching facilities in our hospital, therefore the main stress was on practical nursing in the wards and, because of the small number of nurses, this practical training was well supervised. Most of the cleaning was also done by the nurses, including the scrubbing of the lavatories and bed-pans, the ward servant only doing the heavy work. This was in contrast with the practice in most hospitals in Singapore where a ward servant did, and still does, many duties for the patient which normally, overseas, are done by nurses. Although we disliked these duties, I can see now that the hospital taught us a particularly valuable type of nursing. The nurse was expected to do everything for the patient; close personal contact and care, and not only technical skill, were considered to be the essence of nursing. Each of our patients received a great deal of individual attention. Some of the chronic patients were in the hospital for many months lying on solid iron beds without mattresses. One day I overheard one of the medical consultants of the hospital say to the Medical Officer-in-Charge, "I give real credit to your nurses. Look at this skinny patient lying on a hard bed without a bed sore!"

As well as practical training, lectures were given by the doctors and sisters about two or three times a week. At that time there was no Preliminary Training School, therefore we began ward duty at once. The length of training was three and a half years, after which we received two certificates: one a Hospital Certificate for general nursing of "Women and Children"; the other a Government Certificate for Midwives. There was no official register of nurses in Singapore until 1950; before this the Hospital Certificates (except for midwives) were the only qualifications a nurse possessed. In consequence there were continual difficulties in various parts of the country concerning the recognition of these certificates, each hospital thinking that its own certificate was the best.

Secondly, in addition to the practical emphasis in our training and the stress on direct personal care of our patients, the hospital tried to instil in us a Christian attitude towards suffering. The Christian values of sympathy, understanding and helpfulness to those in trouble no matter who they were, arising as they do from our belief in a God of love and compassion, were very different from many local points of view. Under the Asian traditional system help would always be given to those of one's family, clan or group, but less concern was felt about strangers. This could lead to a lack of care for, and sometimes indifference to, those who were outside this circle. In daily life we saw examples of this lack of concern—a crowd gazing without interest at the struggles of a man drowning in the canal or in the harbour; the lack of care for the handicapped, the blind, the deaf, the deformed and the mentally deficient. Fortunately, there have always been exceptions to this attitude, and now an increasing number are actively concerned about these things; but there are few fields in which the Christian way of life is more obviously distinct from others than in its attitude towards suffering.

The war in Europe had been going on for some months before I entered nursing. Our teacher used to tell us how good and brave the soldiers were, giving their lives for their country, but we were not interested in a war which sounded unreal to us. Europe seemed very far away from Singapore. There had been rumours for some time that the Japanese intended to invade Malaya. Six months before the war broke out many of my Japanese classmates had left Singapore for their homeland, and other parents living overseas were anxious to take their children away from school. Later in 1941 rumours of invasion grew stronger. The public were told how and where to dig air-raid shelters and there was an appeal for blood donors. Our medical officer summoned us to the matron's office and inquired how many of us were willing to give or had given blood to the blood bank. She was very angry when she discovered that I was the only one who had volunteered, and that, not as a member of the St Andrew's Mission staff, but as a Girl Guide. In those days many Chinese were not willing to give blood, as they believed it would weaken their health.

More troops arrived daily and Singapore swarmed with soldiers some of whom were very young and handsome. The thought that these young men were coming here perhaps to die made me very sad. In the hospital there was nothing much to prepare, but we had been warned to vacate the building at a moment's notice, as it was very near a large gas container. We had no air-raid shelter except a ground-floor room which was opposite the Children's Ward and next to the Outpatients Department. In this place we slept on many nights. All the nursing staff had to attend air-raid precaution (ARP) drill, at which we were taught how to put out incendiary bombs.

In all the temples and churches people were praying for peace, but I, in my innocence, prayed for war. I wanted to see what it was like and like many others in the community I thought that war would solve some of our problems, especially that of the colour bar, which was very marked in those days. For instance, during the early campaign of Malaya, someone wrote to the local press asking the Government to supply a special bus for Europeans only, as the Asians were filthy. I remember how angry the local people were. We might be working in the same office or hospital, but once the work was over, Europe and Asia did not mix. Looking back now, I see that the Japanese war did something good—it brought about a closer relationship between Europe and Asia than had ever existed before.

On 6 December 1941, I had been on morning duty and when I came off at 2 p.m. my roommates insisted that I should pack an emergency bag instead of taking my usual siesta. I refused because I thought it was silly. No one knew when war was likely to come, so why worry about it? Anyway my final examination was to take place in two days' time. I had spent just over two years in the hospital and as a war-time concession I was allowed to sit now for my final exam for general nursing. I was very grateful for this chance and I wanted to do well. So the rumours of war meant nothing to me. I was studying hard when one of my friends suggested that we should go to the New World Amusement Park.

"You have been studying too much and I think you need a break; besides, you will be going on night duty," said my friend.

The amusement park was crowded with soldiers. Window shopping was very popular with us as we never seemed to have much money. Two soldiers trailed behind us.

"Where are you going and who are you?"

"We are women from Singapore."

"I can see that," one said. "Can we take you out?"

"Sorry, no."

"Then can we write?" We gave them our hospital address.

Looking at the address one of them exclaimed, "You are nurses?"

Then they told us how unbearable life in Singapore sometimes seemed to them. Their pay was very small and they could not afford to take out a European girl; anyhow, these girls refused to go out with them. They were very far from their homes and their friends. The civilians of their own race in Singapore despised them and referred to them as common soldiers. They had no chance of meeting any decent Asian girls and if they were seen out with any of them they were despised both by their own kind and also by the Asians, and the girl herself would be condemned as well. They felt lonely and depressed and to console themselves they took to drink, and if they became drunk they were arrested. My heart went out to them; I had lost my home and I knew how they felt. Before we could end our tales of woe, we heard a commotion; all soldiers had to return to barracks at once. The first Japanese convoy movements had been seen during the afternoon—it was on 6 December—and the troops were being recalled. So we said goodbye to our soldier friends, and as our late passes were only valid till

10 p.m. we decided to return to the hospital. All the way home we thought of these two poor soldiers who might be killed at any time. The next day to our great surprise we each received a letter—my first personal letter from a young man.

On 7 December I went on night duty feeling rather tired because I had had to work in the morning as well. My roommates had their emergency bags packed ready for war and that night in our chapel service there had been a prayer for the peace of the world. I was in charge of an adult medical ward, which also contained a few babies. By 11.30 p.m. all my patients were asleep and the ward was very quiet. Then a baby began to cry and although I did everything to quieten her, she cried all the more; so I picked her up and wandered into the next ward. My friend Grace was having a cup of coffee there and she began to talk about the war.

"Don't smile, Janet, it is serious. My brother-in-law was on his way to Borneo this morning when he was ordered back."

"I am not worrying about the war but I am afraid of my exams tomorrow."

My baby patient was fast asleep. I looked out of the windows and saw Singapore sparkling with lights and thought it was silly to think of war when it was all so quiet and peaceful. At 4 a.m. my junior nurse inquired whether I wanted to start washing the patients; but before I could answer her I heard the sound of planes. We looked at each other.

"It sounds like war," I said.

"War or no war, the work must go on," she replied.

I had almost finished preparing the trays for the morning nurses when I heard more planes and this time they seemed to be coming nearer. I left my work and looked out of the windows.

"Look at those planes, they are letting out fireworks," I said to the nurse who was standing next to me. Then suddenly the siren sounded.

War

December 1941–February 1942

The first bombs hit Singapore at 4 a.m. on 8 December 1941. I saw the senior nurse moving her patients to the ground floor and I shouted to her, "Grace, please wait for me. I must wake my roommates."

I ran up to the third floor. "Wake up, Mary, war has come." Then I turned on the lights and left quickly for my ward and began moving my patients to the ground floor where there was better protection. I was transferring my last patient when the matron appeared in her dressing-gown looking very angry and said sternly to me, "Nurse, what do you think you are doing?"

"I am sorry, Matron, I thought it was war."

"You imagine too much, it is only a practice."

Feeling very foolish and let-down I started moving my patients back to the ward. Singapore was still sparkling with lights. After chapel and breakfast, at 8.30 a.m., my friends and I got ready for our hospital examination and war was forgotten. About noon one of the nurses came back crying, saying that her house had collapsed. We crowded round her asking endless questions. She did not know the details, but she was told it was due to bombing. We became excited and just then Matron came out from her room and told us that war had been declared between Japan and the Allies. I was anxiously waiting for four o'clock to come so that I could go and find out for myself whether this was true.

For the next few days we talked of nothing else.

One evening as I entered the nurses' room for tea a few nurses who had been my schoolmates shouted, "Three cheers for CEZ," and not knowing why they were cheering, I joined in. Then I noticed the list of examination results on the blackboard. I had passed my exams for the Hospital Certificate and had done quite well. I hurried to the school and before I reached Miss Kilgour's house, she came out to meet me and congratulated me—the medical officer had telephoned to her. My adopted mother bought me a watch and I felt very pleased with myself and thought that life was wonderful.

A few days later we were warned that we might have to vacate the hospital because it was so close to the large gas container and had been declared dangerous by the authorities, so we must now decide where we would go. There was a choice between a first-aid post at St Andrew's School and the Singapore Government General Hospital. The thought of parting left us with lumps in our throats. Although life did not run smoothly in the hospital, we had become attached to it.

Three from my group decided to join the General Hospital. We intended to work there until a vacancy occurred at the Kandang Kerbau Hospital where we could complete our midwifery training which would be interrupted by the closing of St Andrew's Mission Hospital. We did not realise what was going to happen in the next few months or that the war would last so long. In our own hospital, after war had been declared, our daily work went on as normal. I saw no casualties and little bombing was heard, and, therefore, I could not imagine that war had come. Then, on 15 December, Jenny, Mary and I began duty at the General Hospital. Once again I realised how difficult it was to be an orphan. My two friends had homes to go to. As there was no accommodation available at the General Hospital I had to seek the shelter of the school because my adopted mother's house was too far away. On 16 December I received sixteen dollars and fifty cents, my salary plus a bonus. By 17 December every member of the St Andrew's staff had been detailed to other hospitals and first-aid posts, and our hospital was closed and left to the care of our faithful watchman, Ee Pak.

In school, the assembly hall, which was safer than the old sleeping quarters, had been converted into a dormitory where the boarders and I slept. I had to travel about three miles to work. Because transport was very difficult, I asked the matron of the General Hospital if she could provide me with accommodation when on afternoon duty, since I could not get back to school earlier than 11 p.m. My missionary teachers always waited up for me, and were anxious if I were late and I felt I was an unnecessary burden to them. Besides refusing to give me accommodation, she told me that we were lucky to be taken on at all; in other words, she was doing us a favour and she added that the St Andrew's nurses might have to begin their training all over again. It was a terrible blow to feel that we were unwanted and also that we might have to start training from the beginning again. In our daily work we were humiliated by some of the nurses. Besides being called "bed-pan nurses" we were accused of pretending that we were sisters because of our large caps.

The General Hospital was flooded with new recruits who came from all walks of life—teachers, sales girls and housewives, rich and poor, all trying to serve their country. Some of these new recruits had never done any housework—they did not even know how to boil water. They wore high-heeled shoes and dressed as if they were going to a party. I remember a girl being told to fetch a bucket of water. Before she could reach the ward she fell, throwing her bucketful into the ward, which made the sister-in-charge furious.

"Why do you wear such high heels?" she shouted.

Poor girl, she had never done any work for she came from a rich family. How well I knew such girls—when I was a slave I used to accompany my mistress on her visits to rich families and had seen how some of their girls were brought up. Domestic work was considered to be fit only for servants and slaves. All the same I admired their courage in coming forward.

While I was living in the school and working at the General Hospital, my friend Peter, whom I had met at the New World Amusement Park, wrote to ask if he could visit me. I was not quite sure if I should recognise him since I had only seen him for two hours in early December. Anyway he came and went straight up to see Miss Kilgour who brought him down to see me. We sat in the midst of the boarders, who eyed me with amused smiles and whispered among themselves: "Is he Janet's boyfriend?" We sat like two Buddhas, then Peter, realising that the boarders were enjoying the show, asked if we could go for a walk.

"I don't know if Miss Kilgour would allow me," I said. So Peter trotted up the stairs and obtained permission, and once again Miss Kilgour accompanied him downstairs.

"Of course you can go for a walk with your friend, Janet; you do not have to ask. You are a grown-up girl," she told me.

I felt a thrill at realising that I was eighteen and a half and considered a grown-up woman. Outside the school gate, Peter told me of his home and friends in England. I realised how homesick and lonely he felt. He told me that his commanding officer had sent for him that morning and told him to stop writing to me.

"I don't want you boys to get mixed up with these local girls."

Peter protested and said, "She is a good girl and a nurse. Nobody can stop me writing to her."

Peter was in the Air Force and he suspected that he might be transferred somewhere else at any moment. Later he visited me to say goodbye. He promised to write.

"If you do not hear from me, it will mean that I am dead, Janet. Life is very uncertain these days," he said. I had one letter from him telling me that he was in a dangerous zone and then I heard no more.

Day and night we heard the radio announcement, "Florence Nightingale is calling you, join up, girls," and it gave addresses where we could enrol. The Army, Navy and the Air Force wanted nurses. "Why should we remain in the General Hospital if we are not wanted there?" we asked each other. One morning Mary saw in the local paper that the Indian Military Hospital was recruiting nurses. Trained nurses were to be offered a salary of $150 a month as well as board and lodging—a figure that seemed fantastic to us. We received a favourable reply from the matron, who wanted us to come for a personal interview. It happened that three of us were off duty together and so we took a bus and went to see the matron at the Alexandra Military Hospital. Matron Jones was a cheerful and friendly person and seemed pleased to see us. We were accepted and asked to sign many papers including one which read: "I will serve my King and country wherever I am sent." None of us was over twenty-one so our papers had to be signed by our guardians. I was the youngest of the three and Miss Jones told me to remember that I was no longer a girl but a soldier fighting the Japanese. As we were leaving the hospital, she inquired if we had enough money for transport.

She said, "When I was your age, I had not a penny to my name."

On 21 December I told a senior nurse of the General Hospital that we were going to resign and join the Indian Military Nursing Service.

On hearing this, she became very angry and asked us if we preferred nursing black men.

I told her there was no difference so far as I was concerned between black and white, they were all patients. An hour later we were called to the matron's office. Miserably we stood there and we felt as though we were being court-martialled, that we were in fact disloyal citizens and even in the category of fifth columnists. Because we belonged to the Anglican Church, the matron sent for a nursing sister who helped in the hospital and whose husband happened to be a highly respected Anglican clergyman. She said that we should withdraw our applications and continue our service in the hospital.

"You must not resign, you are Christian girls and should serve your King and country."

We stood in silence until suddenly Mary said that we felt we were not wanted and also that sooner or later we would have to start our training all over again.

"Where are you going to work?" asked Matron, not knowing the exact unit.

"The Indian Military Hospital."

"I know Miss Jones, the matron, and I shall advise her not to take you."

This was a bombshell. We thought that if the matron knew Miss Jones we had little hope left of being accepted. However, we rang her up and told her what had happened.

We were surprised and pleased when she said, "Do not worry, girls, report for duty next week."

Later we found out that Miss Jones had never been informed; it had only been a threat to make us stay. I reached the school at about 4 p.m. feeling bewildered and looking forward to a quiet rest. However, the nursing sister had already telephoned to Miss Lane who sat waiting for me. Once again I was judged.

"How could you do such a thing—a child of God to abandon your duty? Do not let the devil win; you must go back to the General

Hospital."

I made up my mind to stand in with the devil and let him win!

It is curious that there was so much fuss over our resignations. Naturally all the hospitals were anxious to keep as many nurses as possible, but it showed an extraordinary lack of co-operation between the civilian and military authorities in the face of a modern war. Later I realised that there was a more disturbing reason. In the Malayan campaign there had been serious desertions by some of the Indian troops to the Japanese and this news had no doubt filtered south. It explained the feeling against our joining the Indian Military service.

On 28 December, Jenny, Mary and I left the General Hospital, and the next day I said goodbye to the missionaries and to my boarder friends at the school. A taxi took me to the 12th Indian General Hospital at Tyersall Park. We were received by the matron, Miss Sweeney. At the hospital, besides ourselves, there was one other Chinese nurse, the rest were Indian sisters. We lived in a neat row of *atap* huts. In front of the huts was a space with a few air-raid shelters and at the back another row of huts which served as dining, sitting and recreation rooms. My room was next to Jenny's and for the first time in my life I had a place to myself. As the air-raid shelters were so spread-out, Matron feared we might overcrowd the nearest one; so to relieve the congestion we were told that three girls only were to share a trench. We had continuous air raids to welcome us to military service and half our first night was spent in a trench. The hospital was a few minutes' walk from our mess. We were issued with gas-masks and helmets, and I felt like a soldier. Our off-duty uniform was white with blue buttons and a blue cape and to complete our outfit we wore hats. Feeling proud of my new uniform I set off to see Miss Kilgour and my friends at the school.

When Miss Kilgour saw me, she exclaimed, "Goodness, that won't do, Janet, you look like a Japanese; come on, let me adjust that hat for

105

you." She told me that the women missionaries might be leaving Singapore soon.

I was in charge of two wards: a medical ward for officers and a surgical unit. The doctors were very pleasant to work with; my difficulty was with the patients who could hardly speak a word of English. We were told to go to the trenches whenever there were air raids. I seldom went but continued my normal duty as if there was no war. Suddenly the first convoy of casualties from up-country arrived, and then I realised what war could do.

Early in January I had a telephone message to call at the school. On my arrival Miss Lane handed two hundred dollars to me. It was what remained of the seven hundred dollars that my old master had paid up; the rest had been spent on my education. I did not know what to do with so much money. My first thoughts were for the boarders who still only received sixty cents each a month. I gave five dollars to the older girls and one dollar to the younger ones. Then I set out on a shopping spree, but all I bought was a Parker pen which cost me five dollars.

Life continued like this until 10 January. I had just returned from seeing a friend when Jenny's packed trunk attracted my attention.

"Where are you off to, Jenny? You seem to be going somewhere."

To my surprise Mary said, "You are going with Jenny." I could not believe it until I was shown the official letter which said that I was being transferred to the 19th Indian General Hospital at Woodlands near the Causeway connecting Singapore and Johore in Malaya. Hurriedly I packed my bag and five of us left by ambulance. Our drive to Woodlands was uneventful, except that we had twice to seek an air-raid shelter. Our camp was in the middle of a plantation of rubber trees; *atap* huts were scattered all over the place. At the back of my room were two anti-aircraft (AA) guns. On the right was our dining room, five minutes' walk away was the hospital which had about 1600 temporary beds.

Casualties poured in, so many that we had hardly time to eat our meals. The bombing and shelling continued day and night. A continuous stream of retreating soldiers entered our camps. Many were Europeans, very tired men who had not slept for weeks. These were the brave men who had endured hunger and thirst, and yet they were called common soldiers by their own countrymen. As soon as they came to our camp they dropped off to sleep, the drivers resting their heads on their steering wheels, others finding shelter under trees or huts. It was a pathetic sight. One of our Indian doctors told me that he was brushing his teeth and throwing water through the windows when he heard someone call out, "Sir, please don't throw water out; I am sleeping under your window."

When I was on afternoon duty and returned after dark, I was very nervous passing through rows of men sleeping under the rubber trees which seemed to east monstrous shadows. Our head nurse realised how scared I was and volunteered to escort me home. One moonlight night as we were crossing the open space near our rooms the men on duty called out to us. We were shown how the AA guns worked, but before they had finished explaining them to us, planes were overhead and we were sighted. When the AA guns went into action we dived under cut trees trying to protect ourselves. Terrifying explosions shook the earth and made me deaf in one ear. Never again did I venture so near to the guns. Back in my room I found that bottles and jugs had been thrown off the tables.

During January there was heavy bombing off Johore Bahru and even more civilian and military casualties poured in—more than we could cope with. Some of the men brought in were thickly covered in mud. I remember a man calling out for water, but the mud was so thick that I could not find his mouth. When I tried to clean him up to my horror his right arm fell off because only a few pieces of skin had held it together.

Everyone asked for water, which had become scarce. We no longer took baths. One of the men I nursed asked me why we were still there, as most women and children had been evacuated.

"Leave us now, you must get away, the Japs are not far off." Actually the Japanese were already south of Malacca.

On 21 January at 5 p.m. we received a message to say that the five of us were to leave the camp. We were too exhausted to pack, so we left at dawn the following morning with only a few essentials. The road was now badly damaged, with upturned cars and trucks left along the way. We picked up two passengers who had been walking for days; one of them had a gunshot wound, but had had no medical aid. Singapore seemed peaceful compared to Woodlands. Once again we returned to our unit at Tyersall Park. The main subject of conversation was what would happen if the Japanese should occupy Singapore.

One of us asked, "Have I to become a Jap's 'keep'?"

"I would rather kill myself" said another.

I always carried a syringe and a rubber-capped bottle of morphia for use if I were hurt, or if I were molested by the Japanese. By this time every available bed at 12th Indian General Hospital had been occupied but more casualties were still streaming in.

On 9 February, the day the main landings were made by the Japanese on Singapore (they had begun just before midnight on 8 February), I was told that as I was the youngest in the unit, the authorities wanted me to leave with a convoy of patients going to India.

"Go! India will look after you; a few of the sisters are going too," said Matron Sweeney.

But I was too scared to take the chance; on land I could run, but I was not a swimmer, so my friend, Mary, took my place. We had little sleep that night owing to the retreating troops, the arrival of new nurses from India and the shelling. By 11 February it was impossible to work; every minute a shell burst or whistled over our heads. At about 10 a.m. a convoy of patients, Mary and the sisters left us for India. We had no help now except that given by the few nurses who lived in the hospital. Soon after the departure of these patients and staff, a continuous stream of retreating troops arrived in our compound. The Colonel-in-Charge told the commanding officer of the troops that the presence of the troops endangered the hospital, but he answered, "Sir, the Japanese are a few miles from us and we have nowhere to go. We have been told to fight to the last man."

Meanwhile a lone plane flew over and we were sighted.

At about one o'clock one of the nurses left the air-raid shelter for something to eat, and I followed her. We ate our lunch under a table. Returning to my room I took my Bible and a tin of biscuits and went to the air-raid shelter. No sooner was I in it, than all the nurses rushed in after me, falling on top of each other. It must have been about ten minutes or so later that we heard a cracking noise. One of the sisters went out to investigate; when she came back her face was pale and she was speechless.

"What is the matter?" someone asked, but she could only point towards the hospital.

We rushed out. What we saw was enough to shock anybody. The hospital, made entirely of *atap* huts, was in flames. Patients were screaming for help and doctors, nurses and coolies were trying to reach them. It was a pathetic sight, men who had been operated upon only a few hours before and extension cases in splints trying to escape from the fierce flames. Most of the medical cases who could walk got out to the Botanical Gardens next to the hospital, but there were many casualties. Planes and more planes were coming over. One of my friends exclaimed, "Look, Janet, that Jap pilot is smiling."

The planes flew so low there was no difficulty in seeing the pilots.

The situation was getting desperate as our only way out was blocked by burning debris. Someone said we were going to be burned alive and this thought made us even more desperate. Guided by an Indian soldier, most of us finally found a way of escape. We jumped over a large monsoon drain and got into a waiting military truck which drove us to the Government General Hospital. Dirty and muddy, we were ushered towards the matron's office. I refused to go in as only a few months before she had been so hostile to me. We were given nightdresses and the necessary essentials by the Red Cross, and were put up in Ward 5. In this hospital I knew a few nurses who had collected clothes and various articles which I shared with my refugee friends. We had lost all our belongings. My only remaining possessions were a chain and a cross, a Parker pen, two photographs and one hundred and fifty dollars which Jenny had made me put into a stocking and tie around my waist.

The next day, the 12 February, I was posted to Outram Road School which had been converted into a first-aid post. Except for an Indian dresser, I had no other help. Some patients had been in this place for days without a wash. There were not enough beds for all and some casualties had to be left on the floor. The Indian dresser and I did what we could, giving injections of morphia and covering bodies. The dead and the living lay side by side.

At noon on Friday, 13 February, I had a telephone call from our unit matron who told me that I was to be ready at two o'clock.

"Where are we going to, Matron?"

"I do not know, it is a military secret."

Upset at leaving so many wounded, I made my way to my quarters. Around 2 p.m., carrying only the barest essentials, I stepped into a hospital ambulance which was crammed with civilian and military nurses. There was an endless stream of people heading for the docks, a most pathetic sight—men and women and small children with fear in their eyes, struggling with bundles of treasured belongings. Much destruction could be seen as a result of the previous week's bombing and I could still hear the explosion of Japanese bombs and the sound of our AA guns.

As we made our way towards the wharf, I knew that I was being evacuated by ship, most probably to India. A few launches had bravely docked alongside the wharf, receiving frantic evacuees who had managed to get passages. Someone pointed to a ship which was anchored off Singapore roads—it was the SS *Kuala*. I climbed into the waiting launch together with other members of the nursing staff and as we moved towards the ship, there was heavy bombing on the wharf; which wounded and killed many people. Several launches full of evacuees capsized—probably few of the people on them survived. We arrived at the boat and mechanically I moved up the gangway.

The *Kuala*, a small ship of the Straits Steamship Company, was only about 954 tons gross. She had already helped in the evacuation of Penang Island early in the Malayan campaign, and like many other ships of her size had had some exciting experiences. All day long on 13 February she had been lying off Singapore, taking passengers from launches and sampans until finally she had about five hundred people on board, half of whom were women and children. Once on board the ship, I pulled Jenny along and we made our way to a cabin, in which eight of us were quartered. Some of the nurses had only just arrived in Singapore.

As one of them said, "We came to drop our luggage and here we go again."

After I had seen my cabin, I sat on deck reading the Governor's speech in one of the Singapore newspapers: "Singapore must not and shall not fall!" I sat with three nurses, all in white uniforms, all talking about Singapore. I had just left them for a moment, when I heard someone shouting, "Janet is dead," and rushing back I saw to my horror one of the nurses in a white uniform lying on the deck. A stray bomb splinter had pierced her head and she had died instantly.

At about 5 p.m. the *Kuala* slowly slipped away and nosed towards the open sea. My heart was very sad and I lingered on deck to watch Singapore melt away into the horizon. Only a few weeks before, she had stood sparkling like a gem; now tragically she belched smoke between flashes of fire, her harbour had become the graveyard of many twisted wrecks that had once been proud ships. By nightfall we had left the smoke-covered city behind and the sky was only lit by fires blazing on the oil-tank islands of Bukum, Sambu and Sebarok. We had very little sleep that night. The heat, the unmistakable smell of human beings crowded together, the incessant droning of the ship's engines, the wailing children, and the fear which gripped us in this turmoil, made our nerves jumpy. On deck an unfortunate crowd was huddled together. Hushed voices, broken by an occasional nervous cough or by the intermittent wail of a baby, suggested an atmosphere of impending disaster.

When dawn came we saw that we were anchored off a small island, no doubt in the belief that the ship would be less noticeable there in daylight than in the open sea. Later we learned that it was Pompong Island at the northern end of the Lingga group about ninety miles from Singapore. It was uninhabited and was covered with jungle interspersed with faces of rock rising to several hundred feet. Close by and nearer the shore was another boat, the *Tien Kwang*; farther away was a much larger one, the *Kung Wo*, which was down at the stern and sinking.

Breakfast next morning was uneventful, but I remember a little girl next to me saying, "Mummy, take me home, we can never reach India; please, Mummy, let's go home."

Most of the morning was taken up trying to camouflage the ship.

LEFT *"We wore sarongs and bathed in an open space as there were no bathrooms available for the boarders."* We also took this opportunity to wash our clothes; I am seated on the right.
(©Joy Seah)

PRECEDING PAGE *Child slaves* (mui tsai) *freed from bondage in Hong Kong, c. 1930.* (©Anti-Slavery International)

BELOW *I am seated (extreme right) with some borders from the CEZMS school.* (©Joy Seah)

RIGHT *"One of the teachers thought it was a good idea for me to join the Girl Guides because one evening she had found me loitering in the garden watching the Guides with interest. Some visitor gave me two yards of brown material for my uniform which matron helped me to cut out and sew. The Girl Guides were then holding an exhibition of handwork, and it was with mixed feelings that I found my uniform among the exhibits."* (©Janet Lim)

BELOW *"At this time [1934] the school had about 300 pupils, most of whom were Chinese. The classrooms...were on the ground floor of the main building. It was old and spacious with large rooms and very high ceilings. You entered it through a porch which led into an open hall with four classrooms opening off it, above which were the missionaries' quarters."* (©St Margaret's Primary School)

ABOVE *I travelled over the Causeway (pictured here in 1937) from Singapore to Malaya on several occasions as a slave girl with my master and his family, and was based not far from the Causeway as a nurse at the time of the Japanese invasion.* (©National Archives of Singapore)

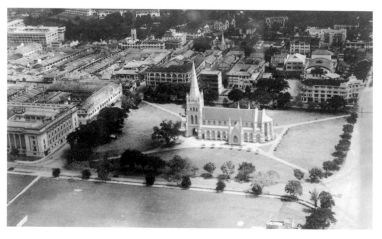

ABOVE *"Once outside the hospital I could not find my way...I saw a bus coming and without knowing which way it was going I got in, and as we passed the cathedral, I thought I should ask God to guide me home. But after praying in the cathedral for about an hour I thought it was odd that I still could not find my way and once outside the church I began to wonder if God was really there."* St Andrew's Cathedral. (©National Archives of Singapore)

ABOVE MAIN *"I was in standard five, at the age of fourteen, when I was allowed for the first time in my life to go to a cinema... The thrill I felt, the wonder of the large picture-hall and the beautiful curtain nearly took my breath away."* Capitol Theatre, seen here c. 1948. (©Lim Kheng Chye/National Archives of Singapore) INSET *The interior of Capitol Theatre.* (©National Archives of Singapore)

RIGHT *Chinatown was once the centre of Chinese slave traffic in Singapore. Pagoda Street was unofficially known to the Chinese as Kwong Hup Yuen Lo (Kwong Hup Yuen Street), named after a slave trader who lived in house number 37. Pictured here is an unidentified street in Singapore's Chinatown, c. 1930.* (©National Archives of Singapore)

RIGHT *Doing the rounds at St Andrew's Mission Hospital after the War in my position as Matron. I was the first Asian nurse to be promoted to the position of matron in Singapore.* (©Janet Lim)

LEFT "[*The St Andrew's Mission Hospital*] *was a three-storied building which stood in the most congested area of Singapore... The main wards, except for a children's ward, were on the first floor of the building, so was the delivery room and the operating theatre. The staff and nurses were housed on the second floor, and the chapel was on the same story. The best part of the building was the flat roof where the tubercular children were given a sun-bath every morning and where the staff could also relax when off duty.*" (©Janet Lim)

ABOVE *The first Japanese landed on the island of Singapore just before midnight on 8 February 1942. By 11 February it was impossible to work; every minute a shell burst or whistled over our heads. On 12 February I was posted to Outram Road School, which had been converted into a first-aid post, and the following day I was evacuated from Singapore aboard the SS* Kuala.
(©National Archives of Singapore)

RIGHT *Doris Lim (left) and I (right) feeding the geese at Doris and her husband's home outside Padang in Japanese-occupied Sumatra, Indonesia. Doris did not live to see the end of the War as she was murdered here by her husband several months after this photograph was taken.*
(©Janet Lim)

BELOW The SS Kuala was bombed by the Japanese while I and many others were attempting to escape Singapore aboard her. After she sunk, I drifted at sea for two days before being rescued. (©Keppel Land Limited [formerly Straits Steamship Land Limited])

Parties of men went backwards and forwards gathering large branches from the island and attempting to disguise our boat—a hopeless task. We said to each other that it would have been much wiser to spend the day on the island where we could take cover and then sail again at sunset if the ship were still afloat. While watching the men I talked to a lad who told me that he was a survivor from the *Prince of Wales* which had been bombed and sunk early in December. He said, "I lost my best friend when the ship went down because he could not swim."

Hearing that I had been bombed and had lost everything, he went to his cabin and brought me a few cakes of toilet soap.

"Thank you very much, you are very kind."

"Listen, I can hear planes!" Fear was in his eyes. About 10 a.m. the alarm was given. "Planes overhead; take shelter." I was terrified, not knowing what to do, when someone shouted, "Janet, be quick," and propelled me towards my cabin. I rushed in and scrambled under a bunk. Then I began to chant my prayers as though God were next to me.

"For goodness' sake, shut up with your prayers, we have enough noise already," screamed Jenny.

The planes, having sunk the *Kung Wo*, turned their attention to the *Kuala*. A bomb struck her bridge, causing fire together with an escape of steam from the broken pipes. The door of my cabin was blown out, bottles and a chest of drawers came tumbling down. Someone was hurt by a falling bottle but nobody dared move. Then came the frightening cry: "Passengers overboard; the ship is sinking!" I clung tightly to my lifebelt and whispered to Jenny, "I cannot swim."

She looked at me without speaking. I knew then that neither could she. I crawled from under the bunk and saw a man—the young lad who a few minutes ago had been talking to me cheerfully about his home and friends in England—staggering in the doorway. He was holding his arm

113

and blood was gushing out from a wound. I wanted to help but he insisted that I should go, while he stayed behind to assist in the evacuation. Holding tightly to my lifebelt I pulled Jenny by the hand as we rushed down the deck, which was slimy with fresh blood. Another bomb struck the ship and I lay flat on my face on the deck; others did the same until there was a pile of people on top of me. Those on the top were hurt but I escaped without a scratch. When I reached the side of the ship I lost Jenny. I never saw her again. I shivered when I looked at the water.

"Where shall I make for?" I asked the man who was assisting people overboard.

"Anywhere," he said.

In an instant I was over the side, landing flat on my face and stomach. I was dazed with pain, unable to move my limbs, and within seconds I started swallowing water. As I struggled to leave the ship's side an old woman with no lifebelt reached out and hung on to me. Unable to keep afloat, with this added burden around my neck, I struggled to keep my head above water. We paddled with our hands backwards and forwards but we could not get away from the ship. The old woman must have realised then that two could never survive with one lifebelt, so she released her hold and struck out for some floating debris. I aimed for Pompong Island but changed my course when I saw a number of aeroplanes swooping down again. A bomb dropped very near me and I felt myself being dragged under; hazily I remember my bare feet touching the clammy mud at the bottom. The pressure was terrific, everything went black and cold, my head sang and numbness swept over my body. "Oh, God, save my soul," I prayed. During these last years I had witnessed hundreds of deaths but had not realised how the dying felt. Now I knew. I struggled madly for what seemed to be ages, then suddenly I surfaced and the light flashed before my eyes; I gasped for breath. I was bleeding profusely from my nose and mouth and was too stunned by the water blast to move my arms or my legs. Minutes passed. I thought perhaps I had lost one of my limbs, and I was relieved when I felt myself and found that I was intact. The churning sea dashed me helplessly about and I swallowed a lot of water. It made me sick and in between choking and coughing I vomited blood and sea water. When I recovered from this shock I looked about and saw many bodies and also patches of burning oil floating on the water.

Exhausted by fear and blast injury, I reached out to support myself on the first corpse that floated near me. Soon I had two—one under each arm. I drifted aimlessly all afternoon at the mercy of the sea. Though the island was so close, the currents took me farther and farther out to sea. Perhaps it was lucky I did not float to the island because many people were killed as they reached the beach or tried to climb up the face of the rock. Towards evening I came upon a small group of European women clinging to tables and chairs. I left my dead companions to join the living. I asked them to deliver a message to my adopted mother, but they looked at me pitifully and replied, "Child, we are going the same way as you are."

Soon a strong current carried me away and I was alone again. I kept on praying to God to save my soul when I died.

Then I heard a voice, "Girlie, are you alive?"

Too weak to answer I lifted my arms up and waved. A man swam towards me, grasped my hand and supported me. We drifted towards a woman and child; the woman was crying, holding her child.

"Mummy, don't cry. I'll pray to God," and folding her little hands the girl closed her eyes.

"Jesus, please send a boat for Susie and Mummy."

They drifted out of sight. I was distressed to see the body of one of my friends floating by. Just before the bombing she had asked me to wear her bangles in case she did not reach India.

Then out of nowhere two men appeared clinging to a raft. We joined them. Gradually more survivors arrived until finally there were about eight, all men except for myself. The raft was a small wooden one about six feet long and four feet wide supported by four air-tanks, one of which was filling with water, but we were thankful to have it to cling to. My stomach pains caused by the water blast became intense and I felt I could go on no longer.

"I'm giving up now. Take my stocking belt. It has one hundred and fifty dollars in it; you'll need it when you get to land. Please find my friend Mary and tell her that I am dead."

I let go of the raft, but someone grabbed my arm.

"You are not going to give up like this. You are the only girl here and we must save you."

I was still vomiting blood and one of the men, noticing that I was badly hurt and despite the fact that most of them were themselves wounded, suggested that I try lying down on the raft. I did so but the waves continued to dash us about and I kept on swallowing water. So I sat up and held on to the sides, surrounded by the men; I was under water from my waist down. As we passed floating bodies someone would shout out, "Hey, are you alive?"

But no one answered. We were very thirsty. Besides corpses, there were many dead fish floating on the surface and when we came across a large one, I was told to scoop it up for food and keep it till we got to land. I pulled it in but it was big, about two feet long and very slippery. We feared that in a few minutes it might slip away, so we decided that we had better eat it straight away. Someone produced a penknife and the fish was cut up and passed around. Soon afterwards a middle-aged man released his hold on the raft.

"Goodbye, I can't hold out any longer."

We saw him go under but only to surface again.

"I cannot drown myself; I'm too good a swimmer."

Down he went again and when he came up he struggled. Then he disappeared. At dusk we heard the Japanese bombing some distant island. It started to rain but when we lifted up our heads and opened our mouths the drops fell uselessly into the sea. Fish constantly nibbled at us; sometimes they came in large shoals and, although we beat them off with our hands, it only gave us momentary relief.

As we rocked up and down in the darkness, we kept our spirits up by singing and praying; my thoughts went back to my schooldays and to the hymns we used to sing. Over and over again during the night the words of one of my favourite refrains kept coming back to me.

Just when I need Him most,
Just when I need Him most,
Jesus is near to comfort and cheer,
Just when I need him most.

These words gave me the courage and the strength to hang on.

In the black of the night we could hear sometimes a baby's cry, sometimes a child calling to its mother. Each passing hour meant increasing cold and finally our teeth chattered loudly. The skies were clear and stars broke into an array of millions of twinkling bright specks which seemed to delight in our plight. We strained our eyes, scanning the darkness, hoping for a miracle. Suddenly in the distance there appeared a little light. Then it went out for a second only to come on again. We all saw it.

Someone called out in excitement, "A boat! Cry for help. If they hear it's a girl they'll come."

In a weak high-pitched voice I called for help. Each time I stopped calling the light seemed to stop, so I continued shouting. As it drew closer we saw it was not a boat, but something large and black which was bearing down on us. Suddenly it dived beneath the surface, then in an instant I was lifted up—so was the raft.

Fortunately I still had my lifebelt on. In the darkness voices called out, "Where are you?"

"Here I am."

"Where has the little girl gone to?"

"Here I am."

"Have you got the raft?"

"Yes."

Fate was kind to us and we reassembled. The will to live and fear of the unknown depths of the sea spurred our little company to hold together tenaciously throughout the night.

When the grey speck of dawn appeared on the horizon, I looked at my arms and legs and was horrified to see how swollen and lifeless they were. Tears of self-pity welled up in my eyes and I gazed vacantly into space. Suddenly ahead of me appeared a brilliant glow and then I saw my real mother's face. She spoke to me and I could hear her solemn voice saying: "Child, don't be afraid; I am always with you."

With outstretched arms I implored her to come, but as quickly as she came she disappeared. In all the years we had been separated, this was the first time she had appeared to me. I had always tried to avoid thinking that she was dead. Now when death was not far from me, the stark reality of her death struck me. Yet I felt her words had a significance; I was to hang on grimly to life.

The sun blazed down on us and had a fearful effect. Gradually our group diminished. Never a cry of despair or a display of fear when they knew the last inevitable moment had come. These gallant men accepted their fate with a calm smile, as each slipped silently away. Nor was there any sign of emotion among those remaining; each wondered when his turn would come.

An island had come into sight but we could do nothing against the swift current to get any closer to it. Three planes darted out from nowhere and we thought we would be strafed. They circled over us, then veered off in the direction of the island and in a short while we could hear the distant thud of their bombs. One of our party in desperation decided to swim to the island for help.

"Don't go, the current is too strong. You'll never get there."

"I'm a good swimmer and either I'll die alone or we all die together."

About fifty yards away he turned and waved. Then an undertow seized him. We saw him struggle for a moment, then disappear.

Land was in sight but we felt that we would never reach it. Hunger had lost its importance because of our unbearable thirst. As I look back now I realise that the attitude of our group was remarkable. There were no hysterical outbursts, no mental crack-ups. The nearest case was that of an English boy who, when the sun was at full blaze, screamed, "I'm giving up, but I don't want to die. I was married only two weeks ago and my wife is now in England, but I have no more strength. Oh God, help me!"

Someone held him firmly.

"Pull yourself together, lad. Who knows? If God is kind He'll send help."

So on we drifted for another afternoon with scarcely a word uttered. All the time I kept thinking of my mother's image and prayer came naturally and easily despite the fact that I thought God had forgotten us.

The sun started to set and the thought of another night in the sea was discouraging and depressing, for the chances of survival were getting dim. Then just before dusk a small craft loomed against the background of the island. I dared not believe it was a boat; yet there it was in the half darkness and there was no mistaking the two figures in it. I shouted and pointed. The men saw it and shouted for help. We were sighted! One of the boatmen got up and started waving, making unintelligible gestures. We saw them disappear slowly around a bend. A deep anxiety took hold of us as we waited for the help which we felt would now surely come. Then a larger boat bounced its way towards us.

There was no cheering; we were too exhausted, and our remaining strength rapidly ebbed away. When the boat drew alongside I floundered for I could not lift my arms. They lifted me over the side; the others followed. Once on board a strange feeling came over me. I must have collapsed for a few moments. When I came to, I had the sensation of floating in the air and can only vaguely remember being carried ashore. I recollect a voice saying, "Lift her gently; she is very ill."

I was placed on the ground near the beach, and a mat was thrown over my almost naked body.

We were on a small island inhabited by only a few Malays; to this day I have never learned its name or the names of those who saved our lives. Our rescuers came round with a kettle of water, but I could not swallow. Someone lifted me over his shoulder and carried me to a small hut, and there deposited me on the ground. A dry sarong replaced the tattered rags which hung around my body and my money was taken to be dried. A gold chain and cross, a fountain pen and two damaged snapshots, were my only other possessions.

For a long time sleep would not come and I rolled in agony, burning with fever, while pain stabbed my stomach. The moon and swaying palms cast weird shadows upon the floor and, my troubled mind could find no peace. Finally I prayed and. gradually drifted off into an uneasy sleep. I dreamt I saw a doctor standing before me with a scalpel ready to cut into my stomach. My cries of "No, no, please don't do it" seemed to scare him away and then a stream of faces passed before me: my cabin mates on the *Kuala* all badly hurt and struggling for their lives. I called to them and ran after them as they began to recede. But my legs grew stiffer with each step. A mountainous wave loomed from nowhere and, engulfed them. They were gone and I was alone, shouting, choking and gasping for breath. When I opened my eyes a kind Malay put his hand on my forehead. He offered me some quinine tablets and a glass of water.

"Missie, *minum ini*. Missie *banyak sakit*. [Miss, drink this. Miss is very ill.]" But I could not swallow.

Morning was breaking. One of the men asked our rescuers to take us to a place where we could be given immediate medical aid, and arrangements were made that morning for our evacuation. It was 16 February. A junk was provided and we were laid side by side and covered with coconut palm leaves to conceal us. Each of us rewarded the Malays as best he could and our boatmen swung the small junk out to sea. The trip was uneventful but we rolled for hours until we sighted a steamer. It was the Red Cross *Florence Nightingale* out searching for survivors.

On board I recognised three of my former fellow workers but I myself was beyond recognition. In my wretched, tattered, exhausted state I remained unrecognised and unidentified. A woman gave me a drink and asked where I had been hurt. She looked concernedly at my sunburnt body, which was only covered with a sarong. I could not answer her but only shook my head. Gradually I fell into an exhausted sleep and when I awoke someone touched my arm and said, "We are in Senajang."

Sumatra

February 1942–May 1942

Senajang was a much larger island than the one we had first left. It was crowded with refugees. On arrival I was taken by stretcher to a temporary first-aid station. It was a picture of sorrow: overcrowded, understaffed and short of supplies. The able-bodied helped fellow patients as best they could, but this help was inadequate. I was placed in a ward for dying patients, the last stop before final rest. It was a busy place; groans, cries, delirious shouts and death rattles filled the foetid air. A patient died, and was quickly removed to make the bed available for another. Death walked swiftly, silently, continuously, and I waited for him to pause at my bed. But the hours dragged on and I was still only his witness. Night fell, and again the gnawing at my nerves began. It kept me awake throughout most of the hours of darkness. The depressing noises of the sick and mangled were more intense by night and each cry fell on my ears with a jolting effect. In the morning I saw a former schoolmate and signed to her. She came and asked what I wanted.

"It's Janet Lim," I whispered.

Shocked, she turned away sobbing, with her face buried in her hands. I lost track of the days but my schoolmate had spread the word around and my nurse friends came whenever they could to cheer me up. One of them in particular would come and sit for hours beside me and assure me that everything would turn out all right. I remember her words: "You must pull through. You're too young to die. Don't you want to go to India and see all your friends again? Pull yourself together; you are going to get well and fight the Japs."

It was comforting and encouraging to know they were pulling hard for me! The will was there but all the same I didn't improve. We had been without a doctor ever since I had arrived and I had grown much weaker. I had managed to swallow a few mouthfuls of water and condensed milk but nothing else. One day a Chinese doctor came to examine me. He shook his head and inquired about my next-of-kin and left. That was all; no prescription, no encouragement, nothing. A few nights later an Australian sister who was on duty caught sight of the doctor going through the ward and asked him for more sleeping drugs for me. There was a pause, then he said, "That girl is going off at any moment now; why waste medicine on her?"

Indignantly the sister replied, "If you think she is dying, why not give her some medicine and let her die in peace? After all, she's served her country and suffered a lot." I too saw the doctor and wanted to tell him what I thought of him but no words came. I was too weak. I felt my pulse to see if I were dying. Death would have been as good as a sedative, but I realized it was not for me—not yet anyway.

After several days orders were issued that all the able-bodied were to pack and leave. It made me sad to see my friends moving off slowly with their few possessions. They came to my bed and said goodbye, "Get well quickly and God bless you." It was an unpleasant experience for them too, for they were going to an unknown destination. Each day I saw more and more people leave Senajang and I felt lost.

One day a new doctor arrived. Dr K.K. Cuttwood was the kind of doctor who inspires confidence; he was conscientious and worked untiringly. He was also kind, patient, sympathetic, gentle and human. I used to watch his tall, thin figure with its clear-cut features as he moved from bed to bed with a buoyancy that cheered me immensely. He had a smile for everyone, words of encouragement for all and he always seemed to be on hand when we wanted him. His kindness and sympathy brought back to me what I had often been told at lectures at St Andrew's Mission Hospital: "Picture yourself as a patient. How would you like to be treated? No matter how unimportant or ugly or poor or dirty the patient is, he has feelings." In the daily rush with many patients milling around us, it was so easy to forget that we were dealing with people. Dr Cuttwood pulled us back to life and those of us who survive owe him much. I found his example a great stimulus, not only to recover, but to start nursing again.

At last one morning I overheard Dr Cuttwood telling the sister to get me ready to move on when the next boat arrived. It was due at any moment and soon I would be on my way to India. I was still very weak, but I was cheered at the thought of continuing my journey to freedom. We said goodbye to Senajang and I saw that there were four other stretcher cases. The boat was overcrowded and every available space was taken up. A man on the floor under my stretcher went mad and screamed most of the night. He was restless and jolted my stretcher constantly. It was agony for me and my stomach pains started again. My cries attracted Dr Cuttwood and he came over and mercifully massaged my stomach. Our journey came to an end when we arrived at Dabo (Kotadabok) on the island of Singkep. The poor man who had shouted all night shouted no more. Someone had drawn a blanket over his face.

We stayed a few days at Dabo and then boarded the *Florence Nightingale* for Tembilahan near the mouth of the Inderagiri River on the mainland of Sumatra. Unfortunately we struck a sand bank that evening and remained stuck near a swamp for the night. The mosquitoes enjoyed our stay and kept us swatting in the moonlight. As usual, people were obliged to crowd the decks, which made sleep impossible. We had another disturbed night with mosquitoes, adults grinding their teeth, snoring and coughing, children crying.

At Tembilahan, the stretcher cases were taken into a makeshift ward; there were eight of us, some of whom were very badly wounded. We were looked after by a lady doctor, Dr Thompson, who was herself suffering from an ugly open wound on her leg; but she hopped around without thinking of her own pain. I am glad to say that she too survived. I saw her in good health after the war, in Singapore.

Word spread among the Chinese of Tembilahan that I, a fellow Chinese, had been brought in seriously ill. They came each day to visit me, bringing clothing, money and food which they had collected. Such kindness opened my heart to them and later when I was a prisoner I used to pray that they would be spared the ravages of the Japanese. I could tell from the look in their eyes that something was very wrong with me. They were sympathetic and considerate and did not press me to talk much. There was a driver who begged me to let him care for me; he said he owned a house away from the town which he thought the Japanese would not bother to bomb and there he would look after me until the war was over. He pointed out that if I followed the English I would always be in danger. It was hard to tell this kind person that I would be too much of a burden on him and that I had to get to India somehow.

A classmate of mine appeared a few days later. She had survived the sinking of another ship which had gone down the same day as ours. We talked for a while and I asked her for a mirror which she unthinkingly produced from her handbag. I recoiled with shock from what I saw in it, a black and blue emaciated peeling face with swollen eyes and lips. Horrified, I cried bitterly and when the sister came to feed me I refused to eat. Nothing seemed to matter now, since I was no longer the same person. I thought that I would be disfigured for life.

That night one of the patients in the ward took a turn for the worse and a doctor was summoned. He made his examination by torchlight and when I saw his torch the memory of the bombing of our ship flashed before me. I screamed for help, struggled to go overboard and collapsed on the floor. When I regained consciousness Dr Cuttwood was there, reassuring me that it was only a torch I had seen. The nights were always disturbed; someone usually had a nightmare and when he started screaming all the others would scream too. It was more like a lunatic asylum than a ward.

Gradually our little group of eight began to increase and then some were moved forward. My turn came, though I was still a stretcher case. The two men on the boat who used to carry me on and off remarked that they no longer felt my weight for now it was no more than that of a child.

We went up the river to Rengat, about 220 miles from Singapore, and it was here that for the first time we were bedded in a real hospital with clean sheets. All the cases were crowded into one ward, the less seriously ill sleeping on the floor. Nerves were sharp, everybody was touchy and irritable, quarrels and bickering were frequent. The morning after we arrived, the queue to the bathroom was moving slowly. Then, when an Indian girl's turn came, a European woman tried to push herself forward but was rebuffed.

She turned in anger and said, "We English are always first, and will always be first."

"Oh, how stupid to say such a thing at a time like this," said her friend. Then she turned to the Indian girl saying, "Don't pay any attention to her, it is stupid."

We stayed only a few days at Rengat because everyone was anxious to move on as quickly as possible. The Dutch Red Cross provided two trucks and we were loaded in them and made our way inland. We stayed in a small village called Peranap, in a little two-roomed house where there was only one bed for the fifty men, women and children of our party. The stop-over was planned for only a day or two but in fact we were held up by floods for some time.

It was at Peranap that I learned to walk again. Word spread among the inhabitants in and near Peranap that a Chinese girl was among the evacuees. It was quite heartrending to be showered with presents of food and clothing, for these people themselves lived in very simple circumstances; and I knew that many of the kind and generous Chinese had walked miles to bestow their warmth and gifts on me. The food I shared among my friends and my earthly possessions began to grow. The Chinese were very willing to help us, but the language made it difficult. I was the only Chinese in our group but I was not proficient in the dialect spoken there, and the type of Malay they used was also unfamiliar to me.

Food became short and rations grew smaller each day. Finally, instructions were given that civilians were to provide their own food. Ill-feeling naturally sprang up immediately. Where in this small village were they to get food? Besides, most of them didn't have any money to buy it with. I belonged to the military party but even I felt that the civilians might have been given a little more consideration. Of course, the military had done all they could but it was a pity that the situation had grown so critical. I was more fortunate than the others. Across the road from where we stayed lived a Chinese family named Yong who took pity on our group. Mrs Yong came every day with food for me and, after seeing the crowded and depressing conditions under which we lived, she invited me to spend the nights with her. Later she also took in another girl. She would have taken more but for the small size of her house and the needs of her family which kept her hands full. Each night we went there and each morning returned with the food that Mrs Yong had thoughtfully prepared for us.

One day the group decided to go into the village to shop. It was a sight I'm sure the villagers will never forget. They trailed us through the streets like fascinated, inquisitive little children. And it was no wonder, for it must have looked as though a circus had come to town. Tall white men in black Chinese pants, women in shorts or sarongs, both sexes in stained shirts and blouses of an odd assortment of colours. Most of the people had heard about our strange party, but this was the first time they had seen us. The villagers spoke in hushed tones among themselves and one knew instinctively that they spoke with sympathy. Some shopkeepers went so far as to let us have what we wanted for nothing; some even tried to give us money.

News came to us that Singapore had fallen; then we knew it wouldn't be long before Sumatra would go the same way. Rain had fallen continuously since we reached Peranap, and had held up our journey to Padang. Now time was short and it was imperative for us to reach the coast as quickly as possible; so plans were made to leave in spite of the road conditions.

The last night in Peranap left me with a heavy heart. Mrs Yong wept and we clung to each other.

"You must stay here with us," she said. "I have no children, but I have learned to love you as if you were my own."

I closed my eyes and said a silent prayer; I could no longer hide my feelings or my tears. I did not know what to say to her, but somehow I managed to explain that because I belonged to the military nursing service I had to go, because my services were required in other countries. I could not express my feeling of gratitude for her kindness.

On the table the next morning were two neatly packed baskets full of food. Mrs Yong, her mother and the other members of the household said goodbye at the door. We all wept. The other girl and I slowly crossed the road, not daring to turn and look back. Everybody was busy packing what few belongings they still had. I hurriedly gathered together my possessions and made for the two trucks, which were waiting outside. Everyone seemed pleased, eager for the journey which would put us one step closer to safety. We were told that a ship would be waiting for us at Padang to take us to Australia.

But soon we were stopped by a heavy flood on the road. Spare clothes were willingly produced to cover the engines to protect them from the water. Both trucks were emptied except for the sick and the children. Eventually they got across while the men and women waded over waist-deep in water. The roads were rough and difficult, winding up and down mountains and valleys. We had engine trouble, but this merely delayed our progress, as our drivers knew their jobs well. We looked at the magnificent views and decided that Sumatra was a beautiful country.

Almost eighteen hours after we left Peranap, the trucks came to a dead stop. We heard a voice shout: "Who goes there?"

The guards were not easily convinced that we were evacuees from Singapore, as Tokyo Radio had announced at the time of the evacuation: "Desperate evacuees, desperate fools, we promise you a watery grave. Every ship that leaves Singapore harbour is closely watched." They were reluctant to let us through, but fortunately two Dutch captains came up in a car. They had just received news that our party was arriving and had come to show us the way. Half an hour later we stopped at Sawah-Loento Hospital. It was 2.30 a.m. on 8 March.

We were thrilled to see the rows and rows of camp beds ready for us and flung our exhausted bodies on to them. I woke the next morning at about 9 o'clock and was surprised to see that the place was almost empty. Three Boy Scouts, two Chinese and one Eurasian, smartly dressed in uniform, loitered about the yard. But no one who had been on our trucks was to be seen. I must have shown my astonishment for one of the lads came over and spoke in a language entirely foreign to me. My gestures asking where the washroom was amused them and they showed me the way. While I was washing, one of the Chinese boys hurried home for his sister who could speak Chinese. He returned with her while I was having breakfast. Mak Choon Lian appeared to be about my age. She was very pretty and had a shy smile which went well with her soft sparkling eyes. We were both thrilled that we could understand each other's dialect. She explained that the Chinese in Sumatra spoke Dutch or Malay and that only a few of them spoke either Chinese or English. Choon Lian wanted to know how I happened to be the only Chinese in the group which had just arrived, and so I went through the story of how we had left Singapore, how we had been bombed and had finally reached Sumatra; and I told her of our overland trip to Padang. She told me that all my companions had gone to church and I asked her to take me there. When the service was over, she took me to her house. On the way I was able to see something of the town.

Sawah-Loento, standing in a valley with mountains silhouetted against the sky, struck me as the most beautiful place I had ever seen. It seemed to us that we had reached another world. The hospital stood on a hill overlooking the town, an ideal spot.

I had lunch with Choon Lian and her parents, and afterwards she gave me two of her dresses and half a dozen handkerchiefs. Then she took me to the house of one of her friends, where I enjoyed listening to the radio.

We were scheduled to leave Sawah-Loento the next day at 2 p.m. and were to go by train to Padang. When we arrived at the station we were surprised to see the large crowd of people who had come to give us a sendoff. Among them was Choon Lian holding a basketful of cakes, bread and provisions for my journey. She handed me a stamped and addressed envelope and asked me to write to her if the stay in Padang lasted too long or if I got into difficulties. She assured me that I could always come back to Sawah-Loento, saying, "My home is yours and you are always welcome."

Why was I going on, I asked myself. It would have been so easy to stay in Sawah-Loento in the midst of all this beauty and quietness, with a sure shelter and with people who were sympathetic. However, weeks before, I had made up my mind to get to India, and, in addition, I was still technically under military orders. I felt the parting deeply and was restless until we boarded the train and pulled out of the station.

Once we had started, the prospect of getting to Padang and boarding a ship to India revived our spirits. The beautiful scenery was also a great tonic. One man started singing: "Pack up your troubles in your old kit bag..." This song led to another; everyone joined in and then someone struck up the familiar tune of 'I'll Pray For You'.

I'll pray for you, while you're away,
Each night and day, I'll pray for you.
I'll pray for you, till troubles cease,
Then you and I will live in peace.

That did it. The words affected all of us and silence fell on the group. The girl next to me started crying. Rather than stay in Singapore and fall into Japanese hands, she had chosen to get married three days before being evacuated. But she wasn't sure of the husband she had left behind. Would he remain faithful to her? I could see that we would get nowhere with this conversation, so I switched the subject to our evacuation to India or Australia, which kept us occupied until we reached Padang.

It was growing dark when we arrived. The evening was chilly but refreshing after the tedious grimy train ride. The crowd of waiting friends and relatives had no trouble finding our coach as it had a big red cross painted on it. We were escorted to waiting ambulances and were then driven through the narrow streets which were congested with hundreds of refugees, many of them barefoot. Finally we arrived at a big house and walked by twos through a gate. Then we were asked to sit on a row of benches. A tall bearded Englishman came in with a list of names and said, "The names of those I call out are to go to the Convent School."

I queued with the rest, and as my name was called I went to a waiting truck. It was a short ride to the gate of the Convent School where we were greeted by two nuns. We followed them along the side of a tall building, past a chapel and soon reached the school hall. To our great delight, there were about sixteen mattresses neatly laid out on the floor ready for us. The hall was roomy and seemed even luxurious to us after our trip across country. We chattered but we had not lost our sense of living in a state of emergency.

Someone said, "Sister, would you please show us the air-raid shelters?"

"Do not worry, Padang is a very peaceful place; the Japanese have only bombed the harbour once."

"But please take us to the shelters anyway."

"Very well, come along."

Having seen the trenches and noted how to get there we returned to the hall feeling contented and ready for the dinner which was waiting for us. It didn't take us many minutes to settle down and soon we all went to sleep.

It could not have been very long before I was awakened by a heavy rumbling and a terrific shaking. Horrified, I started running towards the door. There were shouts as panic seized the group. We stumbled into the darkness and threw ourselves into the trenches. I heard someone praying out loud and a child crying because it had been snatched from its sleep. No one seemed to know what had happened; no one wanted to be the first to get out of the trenches and go back to the hall.

Then a nun appeared and played her flashlight upon the trenches.

"For goodness' sake, hide that light. The Japanese will spot us and drop a bomb."

"Get out quickly, all of you! It's an earthquake! Careful, that trench might collapse at any moment. Be quick and follow me."

Sheepishly we climbed out. This experience was new to all of us and we were silent as we stumbled behind the nun into an open field. The earthquake lasted for only a short while and then we went back to our quarters.

Our feelings must have been obvious for the kind nun assured us that earthquakes were not unusual, but that as a rule they were harmless. All the same this experience upset our nerves and we talked the night through.

We were up early the next morning, eager to see our new surroundings. There were no longer any men among us, as they had been sent to other quarters. The nuns were kind, sympathetic and friendly. They showed us round and told us that most of the boarders had gone home because of the war, and that only orphans remained. Only two of the nuns spoke English so we used sign language with the others.

After a good substantial breakfast, we went to the chapel. The nuns were very pleased at this, but they could not know how much we had been in need of God during the past few weeks. We spent most of that first morning in prayer.

Lunch at one o'clock was an enormous meal and we were given the good news that civilians and military nursing sisters were each entitled to five and ten dollars respectively from the British Consul or the Military Headquarters in Padang. Later we were to report to the Town Hall for gifts of clothing and shoes from the Dutch Red Cross. We wolfed our meal and then divided ourselves into two groups. Four of us belonged to the Military Nursing Service. We started for the Town Hall and strolling along in a leisurely way, looked at the sights. Padang struck me as a nice place but Sawah-Loento had impressed me so much that no place could be compared to it. The streets in Padang were narrow, in bad repair, and from the presence of cow dung everywhere, it seemed that more cows must tread its streets than people. There weren't very many cars to be seen and transport was by bicycle or horse-drawn carriages.

We strolled past the General Post Office, a modern and fairly large building. On one side was a field and in it was a large group of soldiers in ragged clothing. One of them stopped in front of us.

"Hallo, girl, where did you get that lovely black eye?"

"Don't tease me; you know very well the Japanese did that."

"Hard luck, isn't it? But you should be thankful you're alive."

He fell into step with us and went on to tell us how he escaped in a Chinese junk after the surrender of Singapore. He told us how tedious it had been rowing to reach safety, how hunger and anxiety almost forced them to give up, but fear of being made prisoners gave them strength and courage to keep going. He finished his story as we reached the Military Headquarters and promised to see us again if we remained in Padang.

The British Officer-in-Command was very good to us. Having given us ten dollars, he offered us coffee, and inquired what we would do if we reached India or Australia. He turned to me and said, "What about you?"

"I have no idea; I have never been away from Singapore, much less away on my own."

"Well, don't worry, something may turn up suddenly."

We left the colonel and hurried towards the Town Hall to get the Red Cross gifts. It was crowded and we queued at the reception desk to identify ourselves. We could see the clothing and the shoes; most of it was pretty worn. We were allowed one dress, a pair of shoes and some underwear each. Unfortunately none of the clothing fitted me—I had dropped from 130 to 60 pounds in weight—so I had to go without it.

We arrived at the convent to find a number of the women in tears. It seemed that some harsh words had been spoken at the Town Hall; somebody had said that we should be thankful since if we had stayed in Singapore our heads would have been off by now. All of us were by then oversensitive, and to hear what the Japanese might be doing to those of our friends whom we had left behind moved us, whereas a soft word would have gone much further. It made me think of Mrs Yong at Peranap and of how wonderful she had been to me.

We were very well fed by the nuns. In all there were about sixteen of us. Four of us became very friendly, a Dutch Eurasian woman with her child, an Indian, a Siamese war widow and myself. The Siamese woman, Mao, was tall, thin, seemed rather strange at times and seldom spoke or smiled. Suddenly it occurred to me that she had been a passenger on the SS *Kuala* and that her cabin had been next to ours. When the first bomb hit the ship, a splinter had pierced her husband's lung. I remembered that he had cried out with pain and that Mao had become hysterical and had screamed too. She said that when the ship was sinking, her husband was thrown overboard with a lifebelt strapped round him. He had managed to stay afloat and she had clung on to him till a lifeboat picked them up a few hours later. When he was at the point of death, he was pushed overboard. She could never forget that bitter moment and how she had insisted that her husband was still breathing. She was still constantly tormented by this thought and had little desire to make friends.

During the next few days we were busy sewing and mending so the time slipped by quickly, but once the work was done we began to wonder where the ship was, which was supposed to take us to a safer zone. I imagined that something evil was following me and my desire to leave Padang became more and more urgent. Daily we went down to the beach and anxiously looked for a ship. I had recurrences of my abdominal pains, which were in fact to recur many times in the future.

In spite of the adequate diet at the Convent School, we were always hungry. Food became an obsession and some of the women sold their jewellery to obtain the food they fancied, hiding it under their pillows so that they could eat it at night. One case stands out in my mind. It involved the most beautiful diamond brooch I had ever seen. The owner, an English lady, told us it had been insured for hundreds of pounds; but now she sold it just to satisfy her craving for food. She sold it to a Malay who made a practice of posting himself outside the gate on the lookout for opportunities such as this. I was rather sentimental and I would not part with my gold chain and cross which had been given to me by my adopted mother and had been blessed by a priest at St Andrew's Hospital. It was the only link I still had with my adopted family.

Life became dull and our hopes faded as each day passed and still no ship came. The nuns suggested we should do something to occupy our minds. So we arranged language classes and had daily sessions in Dutch, but our enthusiasm for learning was only temporary and after a short time the classes came to an end.

Before long we heard that Batavia had been declared an open city. This meant that the Japanese would come to Padang soon. We had been there since 9 March and still there was no news of our leaving. Mao remained quiet and kept to herself. I had noticed that she wore a tiny bottle tied to a ribbon round her neck. She never said what it contained but one day I asked her and she said it was a charm. She also told me that she could read the future by cards, which interested me greatly. One morning she spread the cards on the table and asked me to choose one.

"My dear girl," she said, "the future is very bad for you. I see three men coming to take you and another woman away. I see plenty of trouble ahead. But you will have many friends to help and, though you will have to suffer, your suffering will not last long."

I did not take Mao's predictions very seriously then, nor did the others whose future she also read, but it helped to while away the time.

On 17 March at breakfast gloom descended upon us. We received instructions not to leave the convent. The Japanese had landed in Padang. There was not much we could do or say. We were stunned, as we realised that, despite all our efforts and all our sufferings, we would now be made prisoner. The nurses were told to wear Red Cross armbands. At dinner that evening there was complete silence and most of us went to bed early; but, needless to say, we were unable to sleep. The next morning through a window we saw a great number of trucks conveying Japanese soldiers to their new lodgings. Following them were looters, men, women and children carrying baskets from house to house. Servants turned against their masters and killing began everywhere. Two Dutch girls with whom we had made friends came to the convent for shelter. Between their sobs one of them told us that their father, a chief of police, had been interned the previous night. The Japanese had just released him temporarily and had given the police arms to protect property.

All that day we watched the looters going from one house to another. Every now and then someone would be seen guiding Japanese soldiers or giving them information. We lived in fear that at any moment we might be taken away like the others but we were not disturbed. Later someone told us that a Japanese soldier on meeting a nun had his curiosity aroused by the way she was dressed and commanded her to take off her head-dress. She did so. The soldier was pleased, rubbed his own clean-shaven head and with a beaming smile exclaimed, "We same." For the next few days we had peace and quiet. We slept in an open hall and there was no way of barring the doors. This made us rather uneasy at night as we expected that Japanese soldiers would molest us. One evening two Malays in sarongs entered the hall. Everybody screamed and we all rushed upstairs in a panic stumbling over tables and chairs. In the midst of this commotion someone spotted a figure in a sarong. A shout and everybody was upon him and we all hammered at him. This surprise attack made our victim speechless, until a female groan reached us, and we realised to our horror that we had attacked one of our fellow refugees. The two Malays had long since disappeared.

One morning when we were doing our mending, a Japanese military policeman, with a European interpreter and guided by a nun, entered the hall. The nun winked at us to stand up and we did so immediately though there were a few English who refused. The Japanese was rather short; he looked intelligent and sympathetic. He made signs that we should sit and go to him in turn to be registered. When my turn came he was surprised and angry and asked me why I had left my country. He found it unsatisfactory to speak through the interpreter so he wrote down a few Chinese characters which I was unable to read. In his anger he told me that I was a fool to learn other people's languages. He said I was free and could move about within Padang. This news displeased a few of the European evacuees who said that I was as much a prisoner of war as they were.

"Isn't China at war with Japan?" they asked. Others thought differently—my freedom benefited them as I could run errands for them.

Before the Japanese occupied Padang we had met a Chinese boy named Eddy Lee who had been a frequent visitor. We thought that we had lost him, but he came in unexpectedly one morning. When someone suggested that he and I should go out shopping, he seemed displeased.

But the nun said, "He is a good boy, and he would not go out with a girl unless she were married or engaged to him."

Someone replied, "Oh! How old-fashioned Padang is!"

A few days later the Convent School was converted into a temporary internment camp and hundreds of people were sent into the compound. Women and children struggled for a place, and there were quarrels, screams and cries if someone had a space bigger than her neighbour. We had to parade daily in the school ground. I was the only Chinese and I was pulled left and right as all the Japanese had different opinions about me—some said I was a prisoner of war (POW), and others said I wasn't. I hid myself when the time for parade approached and was severely rebuked by the nuns.

One morning we received news that those who wanted to go out shopping would be given armbands which would protect them from the Japanese soldiers, but we were also warned that the Japanese would not take any responsibility if the young women were molested. This was more than enough to keep us indoors and we hid ourselves every time the Japanese appeared. After receiving the armbands from the Japanese a few European women did go out shopping but they soon regretted it because the shopkeepers were unwilling to serve them.

The military personnel and male civilians were interned in a camp, but we stayed on in the school. One day we received a letter from the internment camp which had been smuggled out by a bread seller. It read:

"The yellow men have been fairly decent to us, but we have not enough to eat. Can you please help by sending us some food?"

139

While we were reading this, a nun overheard us. She was worried and said, "Don't you see the danger? If the Japanese find out that you have been receiving letters from the camp, we shall all be in trouble."

Despite this warning, we collected a few dollars with which to buy food. Our Chinese boy smuggled it into the camp by climbing a seven-foot wall at night. This he did very often though we warned him to be careful, but he always answered, "My mother has ten children, and if I get killed she will still have nine to look after her."

On 7 April we received instructions to be ready to go to an unknown internment camp. We looked at each other, the same question in all our minds: "Where are we going to?" The following morning at nine o'clock two Japanese officers in a car appeared at the gate of the Convent School. We were ready with our small bundles of clothing tucked under our arms. Slowly the names were called out one by one; we formed up in pairs, no one spoke. I waited for my name to be called, and as the last woman stepped aside, I asked the officer why I was not included; he shook his head indicating that he didn't know. My friends shouted to me, "Janet, you must come along, we have been together through thick and thin."

Fearing to be left alone in Padang and sad to see my friends going away, I chose the internment camp rather than to remain free. Between our sobs we thanked the Mother Superior and the sisters for their kindness. The elderly women and the children were allowed to ride in the car, the rest of us walked. The people of Padang had by this time seen thousands of soldiers and civilians marching to their camps and yet hundreds of them turned out to watch us. The children laughed and made rude remarks. But every now and then someone said a sympathetic word: "Poor things, I wonder where they are going to. Look! There is a Chinese girl. Why do they intern Chinese?"

We marched through the dirty narrow streets and after half an hour arrived at our destination—Alang Lawas. It was a gloomy little bungalow consisting of three bedrooms, all of which were devoid of furniture; there was not even a nail to be seen on the walls. The front bedroom was already occupied by a few friends whom I had met on the *Kuala*. We looked at the dirty damp floor but there was not a broom to be found, racing the second bedroom was the kitchen and next to it was the bathroom with a latrine attached.

I occupied the last room, which was well ventilated. One window looked straight out into the street. Gloom descended upon us at the thought of spending the night on the cold bare floor. There was not even a light. Someone suggested that the Indian girl and I should ask the Japanese officers for the things we needed. As the officers could not speak a word of English, we had to talk in sign language with the result that they laughed and we giggled, until someone said sternly, "Girls, don't laugh and behave cheaply."

Soon the Japanese returned with what we needed except for mattresses, for the nuns had refused to part with these, as they belonged to the school. Our youngest internee was a baby of only a few months— he was well provided for with pillows and a small mattress by the Japanese. The remaining twenty-odd of us who had just arrived had nothing except a few pieces of clothing. The others who were already there had various mattresses, blankets and pillows which had been given to them by charitable hosts, or which they had collected from their own homes in Padang. All the people in this camp were British subjects, most of whom were from Malaya. My Indian friend, Lily, and I made a survey of the house. It was surrounded by a low untidy hedge, with a few barren fruit trees scattered here and there, and a very deep waterless well near my window. On our right lived a Chinese family, opposite a Eurasian family, and at the back was a doctor's house. The Chinese family had a mango tree full of fruit whose branches spread over to our side and we helped ourselves daily to its fruit. Soon many races were represented in our small house: British, Dutch, Eurasians, Indians and Chinese. Mao, the Siamese woman, was still with us, and there were two Chinese who were the wives of Englishmen.

Our first night was the hardest for we were unaccustomed to sleeping on a bare cold floor. Most of us sat up leaning our backs against the wall and gossiped.

"How long do you think the war is going to last?"

"God only knows."

"I wonder how my servant, Ah Ling, is getting on in Singapore?"

"Why worry about her? She is a Chinese."

"She is a very nice and trustworthy girl. She told me a funny story when she first came to me. I asked her if she was married, and she burst into tears. She told me her parents had arranged a marriage for her. She was not pleased with her husband so she made an agreement with him: he could marry again, but she was to remain the first official wife. She came to Singapore to find work and sent back all her earnings to her husband. The first children of the second wife were to be given to Ah Ling when she went back to China."

"What a custom—a wife supporting a husband! Not me!"

Our gossip was interrupted by an urgent whisper:

"You young virgin girls run and hide yourselves, we can hear footsteps."

No one stopped to think whether she was a virgin or not—we all bolted through the window, stumbling in the darkness until we reached the bathroom.

Next morning there were complaints of aching bones. Soon, two Japanese officers appeared—one a military policeman (MP) called Hashimoto, the other a civilian of the same surname. The MP

Hashimoto was a short man with tiny eyes, a bald head and an ugly moustache. The other, Hashimoto Tada, was not much better looking; but he was younger and could speak many Chinese dialects. They chose two elderly women to go out shopping for the camp with the money provided by the British Consul at Padang. After they had gone we divided ourselves into working parties—my party undertook to sweep the garden, wash up and boil water. By this time the news had spread that we had been interned in Alang Lawas; there was always a crowd outside our house watching everything we did. Some of the spectators made kind remarks but others sneered.

When the two women came back there was general excitement in the camp—besides buying food they had been given thirty-three mats and blankets by a Chinese. We all said a silent prayer for the kind donor. As we were allowed to do our own marketing and the bread seller came daily to supply our wants, we had no complaints to make about food. We took it in turns to cook, and I was very surprised to discover how many of the women had no idea of cooking, not even of how to boil water. My assistant cook, for instance, put the rice in the pot without any water! Our Chinese friend Eddy, when passing the house, indicated that he was going to our neighbour's house at the back. There he bored a hole through the wall and through it we were able to pass letters and get information. One morning the bread seller brought me a letter from a Chinese girl expressing sympathy and asking what I required. Later I received a pillow and money from this girl and her friends—a kindness which I shall never forget.

The nights were never peaceful; there was always some disturbance, usually caused by drunken soldiers who came floundering in at any hour. One night the shout of "virgin girls" came too late and we were confronted by four Japanese soldiers who started counting us "*ichi, ni, san, si*" (one, two, three, four). They stared at my bandaged leg. It was

143

still sore where the fish had bitten me when I was on the raft. They wanted to take me to a doctor, but shaking my head I refused.

A few days later sentries were posted at our gate and we lost contact with the outside world. The Hashimotos visited us again, this time to change our money into Japanese money. We were sorry to remember how one of our friends had burned thousands of Malayan notes just before the Japanese occupied Padang rather than let the money fall into their hands. Hashimoto Tada always called me "Chinese devil" and passed rude remarks, such as "be my cook" or "be my wife." I disliked him exceedingly.

Life was dull and lonely although there were so many of us in the house. We passed our time playing a game called spirit. We wrote out the twenty-six letters of the alphabet, placed them in a circle and also the numbers one to ten. In the centre of this paper we wrote two words, "yes" and "no". A small bowl was placed between the "yes" and "no". Two persons pressed their first fingers lightly on the bowl and concentrated on a dead friend or just said, "Any spirit passing by, please come in." After a few minutes the bowl would move slowly, followed or pushed by the index fingers to the word "yes". From then on any questions could be asked and as the bowl moved round the letters and numbers, it spelled out messages. At the end of the game one had to say "Thank you" and turn the bowl over. It was a very popular game because it kept us from feeling lonely.

Arguments and quarrels were, however, very frequent, and could even arise between a child of five and a woman of fifty. Loitering in the garden was one of our pastimes, for from there we could watch our friends passing by and could wave to them. We even—to the disgust of our elders—made friends with some of the Japanese soldiers who passed down the road. One day a soldier brought a squirrel for one of the young internees—a girl of three. She was delighted. British POWs passed our house daily on the way to work; there were always shouts from both sides as the boys made the V-sign. The Japanese truck drivers watched us with interest and one day the trucks broke down conveniently in front of our house. The boys wasted no time crowding outside the hedge and talking to us while the Japanese dived under the truck and pretended to repair it. Then one day while we were loitering in the garden four Japanese soldiers passed; they paused and threw in a letter addressed to the "lady in blue" (my friend Lily). It read:

My Dear Lady,

I am very sorry you are a prisoner, because your country bomb my country. Please give me your photo.

Lily replied:

Dear Pinky [he had a rosy face],

I am sorry I have no photo, because your country bomb my ship and I lost everything.

Your prisoner.

Soon they returned with a packet of ice-cream which we ate secretly in the bathroom.

Then the two Hashimotos appeared at the camp again; this time they wanted to talk with the Siamese widow, the two Chinese women who had English husbands, and myself. We were told to get into a waiting car which took us to the Oranji Hotel, next to the Convent School. Here we were given ice-cream and cakes, and the Hashimotos told us that the Japanese Government would like to release the four of us, but that the two Chinese must first divorce their husbands. That would be quite easy; all they had to do was to write a letter which would be sent to their husbands in the camp. They turned to me.

"Why do you want to waste your time in the camp? Come out and work, and later on you can go back to Singapore."

The suggestion was a temptation; there were luxuries in the hotel, chairs—comfortable chairs, which we had quite forgotten existed in the world.

But how could I trust their ugly faces—far better to stay in the camp than be alone in the free world. On the way back the Hashimotos told us that they would give us a few days in which to come to a decision. We talked it over but none of us could make up our minds.

The Japanese taught us very carefully how to perform the traditional bow—a very low bow means respect for the elders, while a low bow was for our equals. We stood in a row, a Japanese in front of us shouting "Kiatsuke!" (attention!), "Sekera!" (bow!). "Lower!" he shouted. Perspiration poured down our faces; some cursed the Japs under their breath. It was a great relief when the twenty-minute lesson was over.

There was a short elderly Japanese who rode past our camp almost every day. Sometimes he stopped and watched us, but he always seemed undecided whether to come in or not. Then one day he walked straight in, even entering our bedrooms. As he wore civilian clothes we did not know who he was but we named him Tomtit because of his bird-like strut. He became our frequent visitor. The virgin girls were always warned of his approach. Once while we were hiding behind the bathroom we saw him pointing to a withered plant to show that it needed water, and someone remarked that a man who took an interest in nature was likely to be a good man.

The days passed slowly. To keep our spirits up we sang daily. Our favourite songs were 'Terang Bulan', a Malay song, and 'Danny Boy'. Perhaps the Japanese thought we were too happy because soon afterwards we were forbidden to sing, and many new rules were enforced—"Not allowed to use make-up", "No pretty clothes" and "No talking aloud".

The Hashimotos were waiting for Mao and me to decide whether we would leave the internment camp and work outside. Apparently they had forgotten about the other two. We could not make up our minds. We were not happy in the internment camp, and yet the future outside seemed so uncertain. The decision was soon to be made for us.

Yamato Hotel
May 1942

O n 11 May, after finishing my breakfast, I was standing with my back to the window, daydreaming. We heard footsteps and I turned and saw the guards at attention as the two Hashimotos came waddling up the path in their shiny boots. They stamped into the room eyeing everybody coldly. Their glances fell on me. Sizing me up for a moment, they moved forward a step or two and stopped in front of me.

Hashimoto Tada asked, "Chinese devil, where is the daughter of Siam?"

Just then, unaware that the two Japanese officers had come, Mao drifted nonchalantly into the room.

With a smirk on his face, Hashimoto Tada ordered us to collect our things and to follow them. I remembered that when Mao had read my cards she said, "I see three men coming to take you and another woman away." Little had she realised that she was the other woman. We had no choice. We exchanged strained glances with the other women in the room. No one spoke. Mao and I gathered up our belongings and followed the two Japanese to the waiting car. We were so confused that we didn't even say goodbye to our fellow internees.

The small car chugged through the narrow streets of Padang and in a few minutes we arrived at the Oranji Hotel, which had been renamed the Yamato. There had been some changes since our last visit a few days before; I could not make out what they were but I thought that previously it had seemed better furnished.

We were taken to a small office which was under the care of two young Chinese men. The price of a room was 15 guilders a day, food included. The Japanese tried to beat it down. They knew I had over one hundred dollars and told me I could well afford to pay about 12 guilders per day. The Chinese eyed me suspiciously but said nothing. I suppose they thought it strange that I merely nodded or shook my head, for neither Mao nor I had spoken a word since we left the internment camp.

Having settled the price of the room, the Chinese took us to Room 17. There were twin beds, mosquito-proofed like a cage, with an adjoining toilet. Before the Japanese left, they told the Chinese to keep an eye on us, and told us to speak to no one, and to remain in our room. As soon as they had gone, we locked the door and wondered why we had been brought to this luxurious place. I feared nothing good would come of it, and then a knock on the door made me forget my imagined horrors.

We looked at each other. I took Mao by the hand and turned the key. To our relief we saw one of the Chinese outside. He looked at us with scorn and shoved a book under our noses. He spoke but we did not understand. He hesitated, then said, "Will you sign your names in this book?"

Thank God he speaks English, I thought. "Yes, thank you," I replied. Mao and I signed. Then he spoke again.

"All meals are served in the dining room. Breakfast is from 8 to 9.30, lunch 12.30 to 2.30 and dinner 7.30 to 9."

I explained to Mao, since her English was not very good, what he had said. On hearing our Singapore Malay, he became interested and asked, "Where do you come from?"

"The internment camp at Alang Lawas. We are refugees from Singapore."

"Oh, I'm sorry. I did not know you were from the camp. I thought the Japs had brought you for the comfort house, which is at the back of this hotel."

"Comfort house?"

"Yes, where all the prostitutes live. A group of Germans who were prisoners of war under the Dutch were set free by the Japs, and the place they occupied has been used as a comfort house. The Japanese have collected women from all over the country and forced them here."

"We are not prostitutes!"

"Then do you know why the MP brought you here?"

"No, except that they promised to find me a job in a hospital where I could work and stay."

"That's a trick. They will not help you. They brought you here with bad intentions. You must be careful about what they suggest to you."

"What can we do? We're helpless strangers here and know nobody. Please help us."

He thought for a moment and then replied, "Miss Lim, I'll be your friend. My name is Oe Tjin Hoe, and I am the manager of this hotel. My brother and a cousin are working here with me. We will do what we can for you, so do not worry. Don't show yourselves outside; I will tell the room boy to bring all your meals to this room."

Walking towards the window and pointing, he said, "If anyone knocks on your door at night, don't open it or say anything. Jump out of the window and run to the air-raid trench; I'll show you where it is. I will watch and when there is trouble in your room, I will go to the trench and help you if I can."

"You are very kind and I don't know how to thank you."

"That's all right. You are in great trouble and we will try to help you. At first my brother and I thought you two had made a bargain with the Japs to be their comfort girls. But now that I know you are not that kind, we will try to protect you."

Tjin Hoe backed out of the room. Mao and I went to the window and looked out. It was about six feet to the ground and I felt that I would not have the nerve to jump out. Mao said nothing, but I felt that she was thinking the same.

The Yamato Hotel stood on a large plot. The main building was set back quite a distance from the road and on each side of it there was a wing, although these wings were not actually joined to the main building. Room 17, was the corner one at the rear of one of the wings and was the room closest to the air-raid trench.

Mao and I had an enormous dinner served in our room. The Oes had begun to show a kindness which was to remain unbroken during my stay in Padang.

At nightfall we checked the door. Then Mao went to bed while I sat in the dim light thinking. Time dragged on and I got sleepy. Mao looked so serene and untroubled stretched out asleep that I finally crept into bed. It couldn't have been long before a startling knock woke me from my sleep. I sat up in the darkness. There it was again, but this time it came in heavy impatient bangs which threatened to break in the door. In my excitement I completely forgot Mao, hurried to the window, pushed it open, and scrambled over the ledge. The fall was hardly noticeable and I reached the air-raid shelter breathless, after a sprint which my shadow must have envied.

Straining my ears for sounds above the pulsations in my throat, I remembered Mao; God only knew what they might be doing to her. I felt ashamed at having deserted her. I leaned against a prop and wept in the dark. There was no going back; I was terrified and clung to the prop while insects buzzed around me.

I thought of Tjin Hoe and peered into the darkness. After a few moments I thought I heard a movement by the toilet block just opposite

151

the shelter, I told myself that it must be he, for no one else would loiter there at this hour. Minutes ticked away. This waiting was unbearable and I wanted to scream. Finally to my great relief Tjin Hoe appeared. He carried a torch and spoke softly, saying that it was now safe to go back.

We found Mao huddled in the bathroom. She managed a half smile, but couldn't hide her terror. Fortunately the Japanese, hearing no sound, had not forced the door.

Tjin Hoe said, "You had better move to another room. It is too dangerous for you to sleep here tonight. They might come back."

We hurried down the path and he let us into Room 9.

"There is a Swedish lad in the next room, and I'm sure he'll sympathise with you. But if the Japs start questioning him he might let out that you have slept in this room, so be very quiet."

"Do you know who was knocking?" I asked.

"Don't worry about that now. We'll find out in the morning. Try to get some sleep."

The experience had so unnerved us that Mao and I talked in hushed tones for a very long time. But finally we managed to get a few hours' sleep.

After breakfast we went back to Room 17. Tjin Hoe had been watching and appeared shortly after to greet us with a confident, cheerful smile. He told us it was MP Hashimoto who had tried to gain entrance to our room.

An Indian interpreter accompanied the Kempetai who became furious when his knocking went unanswered. Calling for a drink to be served him on our porch, he had ordered a hotel boy to bang on our door. But seeing how unrewarding this was, the interpreter had finally persuaded him to give up and go home.

"Mr Oe," I said, "I have decided it would be safer in the internment camp if we can go back to it."

"I don't think you can do that," he replied, "but why don't you ask the Kempetai to give you a permit to stay with Chinese friends? I went home early this morning and told my mother and sisters about you and they said you could stay with them if you can obtain your freedom. Otherwise it would be too risky."

"But if I went to stay with them, where would Mao go?"

"We'll think up something for her later. First try to get your permit."

Poor Mao did not understand what we were saying. She looked on intently but made no attempt to join in the conversation.

"You must come now and meet my brother and cousin and I'll show you as much as I can of the grounds," said Tjin Hoe.

Mao agreed to keep watch and warn us if she saw the Hashimotos coming.

We hurried to Oe's quarters, which had been an old storeroom. It stood just to the left of the main building. The brothers had partitioned most of it off for their living quarters, leaving a small section for stores. In it were two small beds and some simple furniture. Only one of them went home at a time so that two were always on the hotel premises. Oe Chin Chye was tall and heavily built. He felt embarrassed at not being able to speak to me in English. Their cousin, Te Keng Soon, spoke fluent English and had an alert mind. He was thin and tall and talked with assurance.

We were sitting in their small crowded quarters getting better acquainted when we heard the familiar tramp of Japanese boots outside. I asked Tjin Hoe what they were doing and he explained that they were visiting the women at the back of the hotel who were used as comfort girls. I shivered when I heard this. This could be my fate and if so I felt that death would be the only way out.

I was halfway back to my room when Mao called out that MP

Hashimoto was coming. He was just getting out of his car. I ran quickly and reached the room unnoticed. We waited for the knock on the door, which came a few minutes later. Hashimoto had arrived with the Indian interpreter and Mao and I bowed low before them. It was obvious from his smile that he was pleased. We were told by the interpreter that he had come to invite us to a cinema.

"We're sorry but it is impossible for us to go. I shall be most grateful if you could take us back to the camp. My friends in the camp would think little of us if we went about enjoying ourselves while they didn't even have a bed to sleep on."

"Ah, but orders have been given to have beds made for the internees," came the reply through the interpreter.

"Nevertheless, we cannot go to the show with you."

"But why do you refuse? You insult me when I have come to try to make your stay more comfortable."

"I am sorry, we do not mean to insult you; we thank you very much for inviting us to go to the cinema with you, but we cannot go."

It was not easy to refuse and yet keep him in a good humour. We answered his questions carefully and he finally gave up and left.

Tjin Hoe had been watching and as soon as the car was out of sight he came over to find out what Hashimoto wanted. I had completely forgotten about asking for the permit as I had been so occupied in trying to refuse the invitation. Tjin Hoe suggested that we should remain in Room 17 during the day but sleep in Room 9 at night. One of the three of them would stand guard at night to warn us in case of danger, and for most of the day there was always one of them watching us.

During our stay at the Yamato these three men provided us with more food than we could eat. It was served to us in our room. The Oes' sister also sent me some of her dresses which I badly needed.

From our verandah we could see an occasional vehicle going by as well as pedlars and pedestrians. One morning we saw a truck pulling up in front of the hotel grounds. It was loaded with British POWs who had been assigned to work just opposite the hotel. This made us feel that somewhere nearby were friends, even though they were prisoners as we were. Every morning and evening we looked forward to the opportunity of waving to them.

On MP Hashimoto's next visit I remembered to ask him for a permit to stay with a Chinese friend.

He seemed startled and asked, "Friend? You have no Chinese friend here. Who is he? Where does he live?"

"Well, I don't exactly have a real friend here. What I thought might be possible would be first to obtain a permit from you to live anywhere I could. Once in possession of the permit, I'm sure someone would take me into their house as a boarder and I could go to work somewhere."

"We shall see," he replied, but it was obvious that he was not sure whether I had told him the truth or not.

Tjin Hoe was disturbed because there appeared little hope that I would be successful in getting a permit. He suggested trying other ways and mentioned that perhaps one of the Japanese officers whom he knew might be helpful. We did not know then that Hashimoto was the highest MP officer in Padang.

One sunny morning Tjin Hoe brought in a Japanese whose name was Susuki. He was young, tall for a Japanese, rather handsome with the typical close-cropped hair. His knowledge of Cantonese was fair and he also knew a little English. He listened to my troubles with sympathy and patience. He told us that he was very junior in rank, but he said he would see what might be done for us through a more senior officer. From then onwards he came quite often and showed a genuine wish to help us.

Time dragged, so Tjin Hoe brought us a sewing machine which kept us better occupied than we had been when we merely stared into space. We spent as much time as possible talking to the Oes.

One evening on the way back from their room I bumped into Hashimoto Tada as I rounded the corner.

"Chinese devil, where are you going?"

Ignoring him, I continued up the steps and into our room. He noticed a banana on the table, left over from dinner, the rest having been cleared away.

"You eat only this?"

"If you worry so much about the food I eat, why do you keep me away from the camp where all my friends are? You make promises, but nothing comes of them!" Gesturing with my hands, my anger mounting, I forgot for the moment that I was a prisoner and had no business to be so outspoken. "For what you have done, I hate you and your friend, Hashimoto," I shouted.

Hashimoto Tada stood still, stunned by this outburst. His face flushed, but he did not answer. Then, after a pause he said, "Why do you hate me? I have done nothing wrong to you; I merely came to ask you how you were getting on, but now you accuse me of banging on your door every night. I have two sisters of my own, both nurses at a hospital in Tokyo, and I could not bear anyone to harm them, so I would not cause any harm to you. If I had the power I would help you as much as I could, for I am an old resident of Singapore myself. The Kempetai and I have the same surname, but we are not related, not even friends. I have come today to say that if you want a job I could introduce you to some friends who could help you."

Even though I desperately wanted help I felt I could not trust him. Eventually he left, saying he would call again soon to see if I had changed my mind.

I was very much in need of advice and of someone to confide in. The Oes had offered to do everything they could and had always been helpful, but somehow I could not bring myself to burden them with too many of my troubles. Mao would have been the proper person to talk to—a girl, in the same difficult position as myself—but during the last few days she had not behaved naturally. She said little and went about in a carefree way. Daily she meandered about the grounds gathering nuts, which she always brought back to our room and put in a corner; then she would sit on the floor and pound them open with a big rock. She never seemed to tire of eating them.

One day when she was out gathering nuts, a Japanese who had been watching her mistook her for a comfort girl. What he said to her I do not know, as he spoke in Japanese. I was sitting on the verandah when I heard the commotion. I dashed out to help her. The Japanese was pulling her after him as I grabbed her by the hand. We ran back to our room and slammed the door behind us. I gave her a good talking to, telling her to be more careful. She objected to this reprimand and told me in the course of our conversation that she had been unbalanced and had spent about a year in a mental hospital in Singapore. She had been engaged to a Siamese boy to whom her parents had objected and in time they had charmed her and she had slowly lost her mind. Her actions were often very strange. She would spend hours making up heavily and combing her hair or wandering around with a vacant expression. Yet, in spite of her queer ways, her simplicity and big soft sad eyes touched me and I could not help but feel very sorry for her.

On the afternoon of 16 May, Oe Tjin Hoe came to our room and told us that a Japanese officer had chosen Room 10 and it would therefore be unwise for us to sleep in the next one. So we remained in Room 17. Dinner was served at the usual hour and eventually we went to bed.

Banging on our door started about an hour after we had gone to bed. I cannot remember exactly what followed but I suddenly found myself landing on the ground below our window and making a beeline for the air-raid shelter. Then I halted abruptly and backtracked for I had spotted a Japanese soldier in my path and not far off. There was nothing to do but climb over the wall into the Convent School next to the hotel grounds. I crouched in one of the convent's air-raid shelters, but was found by one of the nuns who had heard the banging and had come out to see what all the noise was about. In hushed tones she told me to go away, because I might endanger the whole convent if I was found. However, my desperate pleas for help moved her, so with a shrug of her shoulders she allowed me to stay and left me.

The banging and shouting ceased but I dared not move. Later Oe Chin Chye whispered to me that it was safe to go back. I crept silently over the wall and was escorted to my room. Not a word was spoken but I could feel Chin Chye's sympathy. Mao opened the door and I stepped in, glancing over my shoulder at Chin Chye who just stood there and nodded. Once inside I fell limp into a chair. Blood was oozing from the many cuts on my hands and legs which I got while climbing over the convent wall. I washed them and got into bed but I could not sleep.

Mao and I were sitting on the verandah next morning when who should come strolling up the path but Eddy.

"Eddy, how did you know we were staying here?"

With his usual airy confidence and boyish grin he just said, "POWs," and explained that the prisoners working opposite the hotel had passed the word to him. He told us of the movements of prisoners and internees which was the only news we had had since moving into the hotel.

Finally he said, "Janet, do you want me to buy anything for you?"

Mao and I eagerly made up a shopping list and we watched him casually stroll down the path and out to the road.

Not long after we saw Susuki hurrying up the path.

"Miss Lim," he said after the usual formalities, "one of the high-ranking MPs from Medan has just arrived and is staying with MP Hashimoto. Perhaps you could appeal to him for help."

"Who is he?"

"MP Yoko-Taichiusha."

"When can I see him?"

"I will make an appointment for you and let you know later."

Here was a chance; if I talked to him it could hardly make matters worse. Susuki turned to go, but I had one more question to ask him.

"Susuki, please do not be angry at what I am going to ask you, but why are the Japanese so unkind? I cannot but hate them for the way they have treated me."

This caught him off balance. Playing for time he lit a cigarette. Slowly he said, "Miss Lim, not all Japanese are bad, but owing to the war, the attitude of many people has changed. I wish I could help you and prevent all this unhappiness." Then, as an afterthought, he added, "Do you hate me?"

"No, you have been kind to me and I look on you as a friend."

He smiled. "Then I will see you later when I have made the arrangements."

I felt that Susuki meant what he said about wanting to help me, but I was uneasy because he was a Japanese soldier and had to obey orders; and even if he wanted to help he might have to do the very opposite. Still I left the arrangements as they were and trusted something good would come out of them.

After a brief visit to the storeroom with the Oes, who always made me feel better, I returned to my room and my sewing. Mao as usual was sitting on the floor, in the corner of the room, cracking nuts. During the afternoon, there was a loud bang on the door; we waited, then silently moved towards it to hear whether anything was being said. The knocking continued and Mao withdrew quickly towards the bathroom. Soon she came out with a glass of water and removed the tiny bottle she always wore round her neck. She carefully let a drop of the contents fall into the water and mumbled something in Siamese. She lifted the glass to her mouth and then passed it to me, and I had a drink too. Muffled voices in Japanese could be heard outside our door and then there was silence. They had gone; Mao was pleased. She explained that the bottle she wore had been given to her many years before at a Siamese temple. A drink from it would prevent evil befalling you and afterwards no harm could come to you. At that time I was ready to believe anything and took it as seriously as she did. But our fears were only temporarily allayed for we heard again the heavy tramp of boots. This time the knock was softer and I recognised Tjin Hoe's "Janet."

He was with Susuki and another Japanese officer who was introduced as Yoko-Taichiusha, the MP from Medan.

Susuki said, "Why didn't you open the door when we knocked the first time?"

"We didn't know who you were. We're living in fear and do not open the door until we are sure no harm will come to us."

"MP Taichiusha is from Medan and I talked to him about you, but I am afraid there is little he can do."

"But surely you can persuade MP Hashimoto to release me. All he has to do is to issue me an official document stating that I am a free person. Without that no one will give me a job. I have done nothing wrong and deserve none of this."

"MP Hashimoto is in charge of this area and is the only one with power to issue documents."

"I know that and that's why I'm asking you to speak to him on my behalf. He'll never listen to me, but perhaps you can persuade him that I should have my freedom."

"I will do all I can, Miss Lim, but I do not think there is much hope."

I often wondered afterwards why, if the situation was so hopeless and he knew it, he should have bothered to come with Susuki to talk to me, unless it was out of sheer curiosity just to see what I looked like.

The next morning Eddy came up bright and early with all the small things we had asked him to buy. I asked him if he knew anyone at the hospital who could help me to get a job there. Pay was no object, food and shelter were all I asked, and a place in which to work and live in peace. If a nurse were not needed, I would work as a servant. Eddy went off immediately and returned before sundown. It seemed that the Medical Officer-in-Charge needed nurses but wanted to interview me first. We arranged that I should slip out of the hotel soon after breakfast the next day and chance the risk of being caught. The Oes were not to be told.

Eddy came as arranged in a horse-drawn carriage, and by taking a winding route to the hospital we avoided the Japanese as much as possible. On my way we passed Alang Lawas, and many of my friends in the interment camp were strolling in the garden. We waved to each other and made signs that all was well.

The Medical Officer, a pale, tired-looking Dutchman, told me after a brief conversation that I could start working any time I liked, but he couldn't promise any pay. I told him my story and said I was hoping to get an official document declaring that I was a free person, and that once I received it I should start work immediately.

By the time we were ready to leave the hospital the place was teeming with Japanese of all ranks. I lowered my head and darted in and out amongst the people, Eddy following close behind me, and eventually we succeeded in getting away unnoticed.

When I returned to the room Mao was sitting on the floor cracking nuts as usual. She was really to be envied, for her attitude suggested that she was not in any way worried, and she seemed perfectly content.

I then realised that Tjin Hoe had not been told of my visit to the hospital, so I quickly went over to tell him about it. Instead of being angry with me for not telling him beforehand, he suggested that I slip away secretly one day and visit his family, some two or three miles away from the hotel.

That evening Mao and I went strolling beyond the hotel grounds. We found to our surprise that the sea was only a few hundred yards from the hotel. The breeze was refreshing and it pleased us to hear the waves dashing on the beach. Momentarily we were lost in happier thoughts when a score of Japanese soldiers went marching by towards their camp; quickly we retreated to our room.

I remembered the old Malay man whom I had seen while I was interned at the Convent School buying women's jewellery at bargain prices. I had seen him again once or twice outside the hotel gate. One morning he came into the grounds and up to our verandah. He smiled an evil smile and showed me a document with a Japanese stamp on it. I didn't know what the document was, but he told me it gave him permission to take me as his fourth wife. He added that he would soon come back for me. I could easily imagine some Japanese selling me to this old man, and rushed to Tjin Hoe and told him of my new trouble. Tjin Hoe teased me unmercifully about being the fourth wife of Padang's leading jeweller. Finally he said, "Janet, don't let the old man worry you, he's harmless."

True to his word the old Malay came back a few days later and loitered outside the gate. I ran to Tjin Hoe who quickly went out and asked him what business he had strolling there. He said he had come to see a Miss Lim. Tjin Hoe asked him if he knew that Miss Lim was under the custody of the Kempetai. This made the old man take to his heels and we never saw him again.

Not long afterwards Tjin Hoe secretly arranged for me to slip out and visit his family. It was a blessing to be away and among friends even for a short time. They had prepared a most delicious lunch and I left with some clothes and a feeling that life wasn't so bad after all.

Eddy visited me again and said the vacancy at the hospital was still open and I could start whenever I wanted to. But any chance of getting out of the hotel seemed hopeless. Eddy handed me a note from the British POWs. It was the most touching message I had ever received. It told me to keep on resisting and to have courage and that they were behind me. I cried, and Eddy was embarrassed, not knowing what to do or say. He had kept the POWs well informed about the way in which the Japanese were trying to molest me and this had roused their anger. They vowed they would kill MP Hashimoto if they only got a chance. I was worried in case the English boys might carry out their threat to kill the Kempetai chief, for it would only have resulted in heavier punishment and suffering for them and perhaps in a mass execution. I was to learn later that most of these boys died in camp.

One day I heard a rumour that I was to be sent to Bukit Tinggi, a town about fifty miles from Padang, most probably to become a comfort girl. Tjin Hoe had also heard this. He at once sent a message to his prospective brother-in-law in Bukit Tinggi. Realising the urgency of the message, Lim Kim Son came to the hotel without delay. The matter was discussed and a plan made. I was to go meekly, but on arriving I was to seize the first opportunity to escape to any of the Chinese houses and ask for Mr Lim. Bukit Tinggi is small and people would be told to take care of me. Through the grapevine they would know the minute I arrived. But the Japanese never carried out their plan; perhaps it had never been more than a rumour.

I was making good use of the sewing machine Tjin Hoe had brought me; at least with it I managed to keep myself reasonably occupied. One day I was so intent on the blouse I was making that I didn't notice two Japanese until they were on the verandah step. Startled I rose and bowed. One of them was in civilian clothes; I recognised him as the man from the internment camp whom we used to call Tomtit, and who was the President of Padang. The other, in uniform, spoke in Singapore Malay. Tomtit motioned me to follow him into our room. Seating himself in one of the chairs he said something in Japanese, whereupon the officer placed the other chair in front of him.

Tomtit pointed to the chair and gestured for me to sit down, Through the interpreter he asked me a number of questions and I explained how I came to be in the hotel and told him of my anxiety to obtain my freedom. As I answered his questions Tomtit lifted up his legs and rested them on my lap, and then leaned forward and stroked my arms. The man in uniform, who was his secretary and whose name, I later learned, was Wakamatsu, showed surprise and embarrassment.

What he said to Tomtit I do not know, but the president got up and walked towards our beds. His hands pressed the mattress to test the softness and springiness. Then he looked at me with a half-smile and made signs which I interpreted as meaning that he wanted me to go to the bed and lie down, I burst into a flood of tears. Wakamatsu quickly explained that the president was only asking whether I slept on that bed and whether it was comfortable. Soon after this they left.

At this stage I knew how futile it was to seek freedom by appealing to justice. My spirit was broken and I believed that only misery awaited me, and that sooner or later the Japanese would destroy my honour. If this were going to happen, would it not be better to end it all now rather than wait to be raped? During the next few days the thought of suicide was uppermost in my mind. Tjin Hoe, whom I had by then come to respect for his judgment, sensed this; he always seemed to know when I had some wild scheme in my mind. I believe he saw the impossible position we were in but, much as he wanted to help us, there was nothing he could do.

Mao and I dreaded the weekends. They meant idle soldiers, with drink and women uppermost in their minds. It didn't take long for word to spread that a Siamese and a Chinese girl were prisoners in the Yamato Hotel. One Japanese passed it on to the others and as a result a group of soldiers would appear. During these periods Mao and I locked ourselves into our room. One Sunday afternoon there was a violent bang on the door followed in quick succession by more bangs. We knew the type of soldier who would be outside. The window was not a good means of slipping away in broad daylight, so we used an emergency key given to us by Tjin Hoe which opened the door leading into the adjoining room. The banging grew more furious, interspersed with shouts and kicking on the panel. There was a pause and we heard murmuring. Then there were heavy dull thuds on the door and soon it gave way. Angered at not finding anyone there, they then destroyed whatever they could. The few pieces of clothing we had were torn into shreds and our bottles were broken. Not satisfied with this, they soiled our beds.

The two brothers had been watching from a distance. The damage to the door was repaired without too much difficulty and strangely enough, this incident went unnoticed by the Kempetai.

Two nights later there was more knocking on our door. This time we slipped out of the window and dashed to the air-raid shelter. Keng Soon appeared a few moments later and told us we must return to our room as the Kempetai were making a routine check. My key, I remembered, had been left on the table inside the room, but Keng Soon had the duplicate. He advised us to appear surprised and tell them we had been walking round the grounds. Tjin Hoe was with the Kempetai when we came back to our room and played his part well by scolding us for going out. Tjin Hoe left and Yoko-Taichiusha, the MP from Medan, told me that he was going to Singapore very soon and asked whether he could do anything for me. I asked him to take a letter to my adopted mother, but he said I would first have to obtain permission from MP Hashimoto.

The night after this episode, just after midnight, a commotion started outside our room and Mao and I crept out of our beds to investigate the noise. Through the keyhole I could only see the blurred movements of a group of men carrying a limp figure into the room next to ours, obviously the aftermath of a drinking party. Mao went through her bottle ritual and it ended by my swallowing half the water.

The shuffling in the next room subsided. Then there was a tap on our door, a quiet rap for a change. We hesitated, not knowing whether to escape through the window or not. The knocking continued and we opened the door. On the verandah stood six grinning Japanese, among them MP Hashimoto and Wakamatsu.

Hashimoto addressed me through the interpreter. "I am very sorry I cannot get a job for you; it would be better for you to return to Singapore. My friend, an admiral, who is visiting Padang would be glad to take you back. The admiral is in the hotel now and you had better talk to him now." He pointed to the room next to ours. "Go to him."

So the man next door was a Japanese admiral. I shivered at the thought and looked from one face to another. Wakamatsu looked sympathetic.

"Please tell MP Hashimoto it is too late for a girl to speak to a man. I will see the admiral tomorrow, but please spare me tonight."

Wakamatsu seemed undecided but spoke to Hashimoto. I felt

Hashimato's eyes burning into me, but I did not look at him. Suddenly I was seized and half dragged to the open space in front of the rooms. I fought fiercely but was soon overpowered. I was released when we were under a tree and there I found myself surrounded by a group of Japanese officers. I leaned against the tree weak from fear. There seemed to be Japanese all over the grounds. Some were singing, others shouting drunkenly. Escape seemed impossible.

Then all the Japanese grabbed me and I was pulled in various directions. They started to argue, which gave me an opportunity to run away. But one of them must have read my intention for he stepped in front of me.

"Follow me," he said. I shook my head.

Another came up behind me and put his arm around me.

"Go to that room," he said pointing to the admiral's room.

"Please let me go," I said, swinging around and facing him.

He was tall, almost too tall for a Japanese. I recognised his captain's insignia; his face was lean, hard and evil in the moonlight shadows. Again he said, "Go, he loves you."

My anger rose, and I shouted, "No, I will never go to that room; you will have to kill me first."

Too late, I saw the swift movement of his hand. His blow struck me to the ground, and a kick on my thigh paralysed my leg. I lay quiet for a moment and my head swam. Someone shouted as I began to crawl; then, just as I had managed to get to my feet, another Japanese pushed me and I fell on my face again. The Japanese grabbed my legs and dragged me back into the circle. Again I managed to get on to my feet. Someone shouted as I ran two steps towards the main building. Then I went sprawling on my face as the Japanese pushed me and dragged me back. The argument continued. I started screaming, "Jesus, come quickly, send a big bomb to kill all these wicked men." Over and over I screamed, "Jesus." A short Japanese knelt down and dabbed the blood trickling from the cuts I had received by falling on the gravel.

He said, "Come with me and I will take care of you."

I struggled to get up and grabbed Wakamatsu's hand. Speaking in Malay I begged him, "Please help me, no one else will."

His eyes shifted to his companion and then back to me.

"Run quickly to your room when I start talking to them. I will try to persuade them to go home."

When he started talking I took my opportunity and raced to my room. I fell on the floor and then noticed how much I was trembling. My whole body ached. I was deeply humiliated. As I lay there the tramp of boots pounded up the verandah and a heavy fist banged on the door. I got up, but the room rocked and the walls seemed to be pressing upon me. Steadying myself I shuffled towards the window and threw it open and climbed out. How far I ran I cannot remember, but I know I stumbled and fell, too exhausted to get up again. Lying there I heard a gentle voice calling, "Janet." It was one of the Oes. He helped me to my feet and half dragged me into a tiny storeroom. He found a blanket and an old pillow and told me to rest.

Tjin Hoe came just after the break of day and told me to go back to my room. The night's events preyed on me and I was depressed. I wandered into the garden and felt like screaming. Finally I went to a quiet spot and started to sing:

Just when I need Him most,
Just when I need Him most,
Jesus is near to comfort and cheer,
Just when I need Him most.

But at the time these words seemed a mockery, for there I was utterly helpless and I felt very far away from a God who did not seem to care.

About three days later a Japanese officer brought word that there was a job for me as a waitress. Feeling that it might be another trick, I inquired for whom I would be working and was surprised that it was Fusiyama Taisan (Tomtit), President of Padang, who a few days ago had humiliated me by putting his legs on my lap and by stroking my arms.

I threw my head back and laughed. The Japanese was surprised and asked when I would be ready. I said I'd let him know later.

Again I went to Tjin Hoe for advice; he said it was a good idea as Tomtit was known as a good man and all right to work for. But he did not know about Tomtit's behaviour in my room, and in fact I had already made up my mind I would not work for him. I returned to my room with a feeling of emptiness. The pressure of these last three days had been more than I could bear. My emotions welled up and I wept. I remembered the date and sat down and wrote the following letter:

28th May, 1942

Dear Seng [my adopted brother in Singapore],

You will be surprised to receive this letter and learn I am still alive. First of all I want to apologise for leaving Singapore without informing you, but it was not my choice. Our ship was bombed and sunk after we left, and I was in the sea for many hours. I was rescued by Malay fishermen and brought to Sumatra.

All the suffering I went through is nothing compared with the agony I am going through now. This is my last letter to you, the last you will ever hear from me. I am sick and tired of this world.

Please look after Mama. Goodbye and love to all.

Your loving sister,

Jan

This letter was addressed and left on the table in our room. Later Tjin Hoe came to tell me he was going to Bukit Tinggi for a few days and said that his brother Chin Chye would keep an eye on me while he was gone.

"There's nothing to worry about; keep your chin up," he said.

I saw him off at the gate. I was sick and frightened and far from keeping my chin up. I felt like an old woman and not like a girl of eighteen and a half.

Late the following afternoon, while I was lying on the bed resting, there was a gentle tap on the door. For once I did not hesitate and opened the door. MP Hashimoto stood there alone, and the shock of seeing him made me unsteady, so I sat down on one of the chairs on the verandah. Hashimoto sat opposite looking at me with an intent gaze. He arose and walked towards me and as he came near I screamed, "No, please don't touch me!"

He was just about to grab me, when Mao strolled out of the bedroom on to the verandah. Then he seized both of us by our wrists and pulled us down the path until we came to Room 2.

We were pulled to the door which he opened, then with a quick movement he pushed Mao and me rudely into the room. We were both disturbed to find another Japanese waiting for us.

A hasty look at the room told me there was little hope of escape from it. It was a bedsitting room with a screened bed in one corner and was furnished with a cupboard, a table, four chairs and a washbasin. The windows were firmly shut and the only way out was by the main entrance through which we had come. A samurai sword in its gleaming sheath lay on the floor near to the door of the mosquito-proofed bed section.

The little Japanese motioned us to sit down. He was short and slight, ugly and bald. He had small rat-like eyes and his long upper lip was amply covered with a rather dirty moustache. It was obvious that he hadn't shaved for some days and his bloodshot eyes gave him a hideous appearance.

He talked to Hashimoto in Japanese for a long time. Their voices were loud and noisy. Every now and then as they talked, a finger was pointed at me. When the little Japanese got up to pace the floor, his unsteadiness convinced me that he had been drinking.

Suddenly he reeled over to me and spoke in English.

"How old are you?"

"Twenty-six," I lied.

"Ha! You are only a child."

"Then, if I am only a child, you should help me."

"Yes, that is what I am going to do. Ha! Ha!" He paused. "I am an admiral and sometimes for months I see only the sea and the blue sky, so when Hashimoto told me about you, I congratulated myself how lucky I was to have a virgin. You are going to be mine first. Ha! Ha!"

Anger swept over me and I shouted back, "Then what will happen to me afterwards?"

"Ha! Ha! You will either return safely to your people or go into a comfort house."

I shouted, "You will only have my dead body." I no longer feared this man; hate raged within me and one of us was going to die for I would not submit.

Hashimoto grabbed Mao and dragged her to the door. I sprang to follow them but he turned and gave me a hard push which sent me flying backwards. Then he slammed the door and I heard the bolt being pushed on the outside.

The admiral smiled contentedly and staggered forward with his arms outstretched, I gently pushed him into his chair and sat facing him and changed my tactics. I even tried to smile at him.

He mumbled, "You were a naughty girl to run away from me the other night."

"Oh, it was you. I didn't know."

He nodded. I played for time and appealed to his chivalry.

"Don't you want to help me? Suppose your daughter was stranded far away from home and people wanted to harm her. Then she was rescued and brought back safely to you by some kind person. Wouldn't you be grateful? Just as my family will be if you leave me alone."

"No," he shouted back, "I want you. I am going to have you first."

"But I'm not a virgin. I have a husband and three children. They are in Singapore. Please let me go."

I sat frozen to my chair as he pointed to the bed and ordered me to go to it. By now it was getting dark and he began to undress, until he had all his clothes off except for a T-bandage. I was shocked, not only at seeing him almost naked, but also because his body was so hairy. I flew towards the windows but they were locked. I fell into a chair. He grabbed it and wheeled me towards the bed. I hung on to the chair as he pulled me and jammed it against the mosquito-proofed bed door to keep it from swinging shut. He was pleased with himself and let out an evil laugh. He was now on his back in bed reaching out for me and trying to pull me to him. My eyes were fixed on the gleaming sword lying just outside the door. We tussled but he could not pull me down from the position he was lying in. He was immensely pleased at all the fun he was having. With my free hand I stretched out for the sword, but he pulled me back and his hands tore at my clothing.

Suddenly I was overcome with anger and I sprang on top of him and pinned him down. I jammed one knee into his stomach and my left hand clutched his throat. Because of his drunken state and his awkward position I was able to hold him down. He began to choke and I bore down harder. His face reddened, and his eyes bulged, as I screamed over and over again, "Jesus, help me!"

Just then there was an urgent knock at the door, and I heard a voice calling, "*Nona* [Miss], dinner is ready."

I shouted, "Open the door," and it was flung open. I turned to see Keng Soon, Chin Chye and four waiters. I released my hold and Keng Soon gave a significant jerk with his thumb for me to get out and run. I was almost at the door when the admiral leapt for his sword. Keng Soon stepped in front of him and talked to him, giving me a few precious seconds to get going. I heard his shouts of "I kill you! I kill you!" and turning I saw him brandishing his sword in the air and coming after me. I screamed and continued running blindly. When I turned again he was no longer to be seen. I ran until I stumbled and felt under some trees. There I rested a few minutes and then continued walking until I saw some lights not far away. As I drew closer, I noticed that Japanese in uniform were in the house, so I turned back in the direction I had come from, finally dropping to the ground exhausted.

Much later I was startled by a soft voice calling me. Chin Chye had started looking for me the minute it had become safe enough to do so. He carried a flashlight in one hand and a bottle of water in the other. His voice was hoarse and shaky as he whispered to me to follow him. He told me how they came to enter the room at the right time. As soon as MP Hashimoto took us along to Room 2 he had contacted a number of Chinese friends to see what they could do. Their plans were interrupted by my screams so they decided to send the waiters to announce dinner, and used this as an excuse to enter the room. He told me that after I had escaped the Japanese had ransacked the hotel looking for me, but had finally found another girl as a substitute. They had locked my room and had taken the key with them.

He said, "You must not go back to your room. You must run away."

Escape

June 1942

Chin Chye and I walked back silently and finally came to an unused garage near the back of the hotel. Quietly he opened the door and motioned me in. Inside was an old car thick with cobwebs. The air was damp and musty and the ground soft with moisture. Chin Chye handed me the bottle of water and apologised for not bringing any food. He told me to sleep in the car and said he would come back before daylight with plans for my escape.

It was very dark in the garage, and I felt like choking from the smell. Gradually I got used to the buzzing of insects and to the mosquito bites but the ghostly rustling of the trees outside terrified me. I thought of the letter to my brother which I had left on the table, and I feared that the Kempetai might trace him in Singapore and make reprisals upon my family for my resistance. This added to my worries and I was deeply distressed. I did not sleep but only dozed. I awoke with a start and heard something moving outside. There was a fumbling at the door, which opened on its creaking hinges. I crouched low, pressing my body close to the floor of the car. I dared not breathe. The door closed and I recognised Chin Chye's soft whisper.

"Janet, are you awake?"

I moved and he went on, "Hurry, we must go quickly." I scrambled out of the car and followed. He explained as we walked that he was taking me to a friend's house where I could go into hiding. When we reached a small *atap* house it was daybreak. A kindly looking Malay woman was waiting and smiled as she greeted me. I tried to answer but no words came. Chin Chye filled a basin with water for me to wash. He said that breakfast would be ready soon. I could not grasp the situation, for I could hear whispers in Malay and imagined that people were peeping at me from the other room. I was given a comb and in the mirror I saw how haggard I looked. I was groggy too, as I hadn't slept well for weeks. I was given a big bowl of hot coffee. Chin Chye advised me that it would be best if I hid in the attic; so they hauled me up in a rice sack tied to a rope slung over a rafter.

Again I found myself in the dark in stale and mouldy air. As my eyes became accustomed to the darkness I saw mice scurrying across the floor. I was too exhausted to bother about them, or to be frightened, and I stretched myself out and waited for sleep to come and blot out all my worries. But sleep did not come easily and I kept wondering about who these strangers were and why they were so willing to help me. How long would I stay here, and how safe would it be? A mouse crawled over my body and I brushed it off. Then I dropped into an exhausted sleep.

When I opened my eyes again I heard a man's muffled voice below. I noticed that the sun was shining through the *atap* roof and knew that I had slept for many hours. Anxious to know whose voice it was, I found a small peephole and looked down to see Keng Soon. I called to him and he helped me down. He told me arrangements had been made for me to move again. It was a hot day and the sun was well up. The kind Malay woman took me into her room and I combed my hair straight back, tied a Malay scarf over it and put on a Malay sarong and blouse which she gave me. When I was dressed I looked quite like a Malay but I did not feel comfortable in these strange clothes. Keng Soon told me to carry a basket and to seem to be going to market. Outside the hut a carriage waited; I said goodbye to the woman and got into it.

Keng Soon cycled ahead of the carriage; the driver had been given his instructions. I thought that we moved very slowly and that the horse trotted as though he had been galloping for days without a rest. We followed a winding route to avoid as many Japanese as we could, but we did not completely escape them, and when we approached them I bowed low from the carriage. We were stopped at a sentry post but this did not cause us any trouble. I did not know how far we had travelled but it seemed a long way. When we finally came to a stop in front of a small bungalow, I breathed a sigh of relief that the journey was over.

An old lady was waiting. She was dressed in Malay costume and I was not certain whether she was Chinese or Malay. Keng Soon introduced me and told me to call her Ntjim.

Keng Soon said, "I think you will be safe here but you must stay inside the house and learn to speak the local Malay dialect as quickly as you can." I remember his parting words, "Janet, we won't be coming to see you unless it is absolutely necessary. It is too dangerous, because we might be followed."

I watched him pedal off down the road and thought what a risk these young friends were taking to save me. I had a sinking feeling that I would not be seeing Keng Soon, Chin Chye or Tjin Hoe again for a long time, and suddenly I felt very lonely and wanted to cry out to Keng Soon to beg him to come back.

The people in Ntjim's house looked at me with great curiosity and only smiled shyly. Then a little girl came forward and took my hand. She called me Tatji, which I learned later meant sister. She examined my fingernails, and I thought back to the Convent School where I had had the last opportunity of painting them with some borrowed varnish. She asked whether I danced and I told her I used to love it. She said few girls in Padang were allowed to dance as the people were very conservative.

I learned that there were two Ntjims, both of whom were Chin

Chye's aunts on his mother's side. One of them, who was rather stout, was a widow and had two sons and one daughter—the latter was staying in the house for fear of the Japanese who were looking for women. Her mother was there only on a short visit. The other Ntjim, the owner of the house, was thin, very pale and delicate. They had three sons and a daughter. The eldest son, who was married, lived in his own place, but his young daughter, aged five years, who had a harelip, lived with her grandparents. I felt sorry for this child, whose face was so unattractive, and as I came to know them better I asked whether they had not thought of sending her to hospital for surgical treatment. They did not know that such an operation was possible and were much surprised to hear about it. The head of the family, an old man whom I called uncle in Malay, was the only one who could speak Chinese and was a great help to me in conversing with other members of the family. He was thin, like his wife, and had a rather dried-up look. He moved about slowly, shuffling instead of walking, but his thoughts were clear and he was always quick with his answers.

I surveyed the surroundings. The house was not big. Its thin wooden boards were cracked in places and the roof was made of *atap* like all the other houses in this region. There were two bedrooms, a sitting room, and a verandah. Creaking steps led up to the verandah facing the road. At the back of the house about ten yards away was a well and to the right of this a tiny bathroom. At the back was also a porch, its flooring built of heavy rough planks. It served as a storeroom and housed many barrels which I later learned contained caustic soda, used for making soap. There were large vats on the porch in which the ingredients were cooked and made into soap. This was later sold to the people of Padang. Out in the yard I could see a vegetable bed and a delightful flock of geese, ducks and chickens. Beyond the backyard lay a mangrove swamp and secondary jungle.

A small lane led to the house from the main road which was about a hundred yards away. To our right, a short distance away and only separated by a low unkempt hedge, was another small house. Our neighbour, an old Chinese woman, could look right into our house and see what was going on. Being an inquisitive neighbour, she soon came over to find out who had come in the carriage. I happened to be in the bedroom when she called, so she was told that I was a distant relative, and that I had already left.

There were two Malay men servants who did odd jobs. They were warned not to talk about the new arrival. Everyone was kind and did all they could to make me comfortable. They were eager to learn something about Singapore, for it seemed a Utopia to them.

The old man studied me carefully and after considerable thought said to me, "Miss Lim, you are very young to be in so much trouble. We will do everything we can to protect you. You must stay with us for a while, but it will be better if you remain in your room, for many people come here every day to buy soap."

"I'll do as you say," I answered, " but isn't there something I can do to make myself useful?"

"We'll see, but for the next few days do not show yourself when visitors come. And only leave the house when it is absolutely necessary."

"Do the Japs come this way very often?"

"They have come here several times, but it is quite a few days since any have been seen around here. Now that you are wanted, they will probably send parties out to search this region."

"What will I do when they come?"

"Don't worry about that now. We will meet the situation when it comes. But you will have to act quickly when we tell you what to do."

"I fear you are all being endangered by my presence here."

"That may be so for the next few days while they search the area.

But after that it will not be so bad, and after a while the Japs will believe you're dead."

"How can I ever repay you?"

"Do not feel that we would ever expect anything; just accept us as we accept you. We are very glad to help you, but what we have to offer you is very little."

I felt embarrassed, not knowing what to say, and rather than shed any tears before him, I went to the bedroom which I shared with the two daughters and the little harelipped girl. I spent the rest of the day in this room.

For the first few mornings one of the daughters brought my breakfast to this room. The meal usually consisted of rice and vegetables and a little meat, all placed neatly on banana leaves. I looked for a spoon and fork and turned to the daughter. She smiled and went out and brought in her own breakfast and showed me how to use three fingers to carry the food to one's mouth. It was awkward at first; I fumbled and made a mess on the floor with the rice, but gradually I learned.

The people of the house seemed strange to me. They were Chinese, but they dressed as Malays and followed Malay customs. One of the daughters, however, wore frocks. Not one spoke their native tongue except the old man. I knew a little Malay of the kind spoken in Singapore, but it was different from the way in which it was spoken in Sumatra.

It was boring to sit in a room day after day while everyone else was up and around early, doing the daily chores, so after many days of idleness I asked for permission to help and was delighted that I was allowed to feed the chickens and ducks and help a little in the house. In the evening a steady stream of people came to buy soap so at that time of the day I stayed in the bedroom. Often the daughters would sit with me and ask questions about Singapore. They were interested in how the young people lived and were surprised that boys and girls mixed fairly freely, for in Sumatra girls were only allowed to talk to boys once they were engaged to them; most marriages were arranged by the parents. These girls had never had an opportunity of associating with boys.

A week after I arrived I noticed a man on a bicycle coming up the lane. It was Tjin Hoe, who had just returned from Bukit Tinggi.

"You look like a Padang girl now," he said, looking at my Malay garb and straight-combed hair. "How's life treating you?"

"All right, I like it here. Everyone is nice to me."

He handed me a bundle of clothes, saying, "Chin Chye slipped into your room after you escaped but he didn't dare take everything as the Japs would have found out."

"Are they still looking for me?"

"Yes. They were very angry when you got away. They ransacked your room and searched the whole hotel. The servants had a hard time being questioned by MP Hashimoto and they have been ordered to search for you. It's a good thing I was away or else they would have suspected that I helped you to escape."

"But what about Keng Soon and Chin Chye?"

"The Japs don't suspect them, though they questioned them a number of times. Three days after you got away the Japs came and took all your things. MP Hashimoto took the letter addressed to your brother and later he came to me and ordered me to read it and tell him what was in it.

"What did you tell him?"

"That the letter was to your brother telling him you intended to commit suicide. And I told him the only place where you could do that was in the sea." He laughed and continued, "Later a party of Japs and coolies were sent out to look for your body. As they didn't find it, MP

Hashimoto came to see me and accused me of hiding you, but I had the excuse of having been away. They are not convinced that you are dead and the search is still going on."

"Do you think I'm safe here?"

"Well, so far so good, but you can't be too careful. Things will get better after a while when the Japs who are here now go away and a new lot come. By the way, Susuki called this morning to say goodbye to you. He didn't know that you had escaped and when I told him you had committed suicide, he was very sad and for a while he didn't say anything. Then he became angry and kept saying: 'Very much sorry, Japanese people very bad.'"

I knew that Susuki felt that way about the Military Police, but because he was so junior he had little or no voice in what should or should not be done in administering the area. Susuki and Wakamatsu were the only two Japanese who seemed to be human. I said this to Tjin Hoe who agreed with me; but he added, "We must be very careful even with them, because they are in the army and have to obey orders, and might feel it was their duty to report you if they knew where you were."

He gave me the forty guilders which I had asked him to keep for me and said, "You had better give thirty to my aunt; she is not very well and the family doesn't make much money selling soap, and they work pretty hard just to make a living. I must be going back now. Be careful and stay in the house as much as possible; remember the Japanese are still looking for you."

I watched Tjin Hoe cycle down the narrow, lonely path. At the far end he turned his head and waved. Then quickly he was out of sight and I wondered when I would see him again.

These short visits of Tjin Hoe and his brother and their cousin were precious to me. Whenever they appeared I felt more at ease and more secure. Somehow, they always managed to allay my fears, even if only for a short while. No finer young men could be met anywhere and I owe them a tremendous debt of gratitude. Without them I would have had no chance of escaping being raped in the hotel.

I fell into the monotonous routine of being idle most of the day. The nights were long. Ever since I had been picked up on that isolated little island I had been disturbed by nightmares and bad dreams. I felt sorry for myself and anxious about the future. Had I been kept busy I might have forgotten my troubles in hard work, I would have lived for the day and thought less of the past or the horrors of the future. Still I did as many chores as possible, and as I became more occupied, I began to live again.

One day my routine was interrupted when one of the girls came running excitedly into the house. She stammered that the gossip next door had cornered her and questioned her suspiciously about me. She had seen me feeding the fowl and wanted to know who I was, where I came from and why I was there. The girl had told her that I was a distant cousin and had begged the old woman to say nothing to anyone. Now the household began to look worried and the delicate Ntjim crept out of her room and suggested that I should immediately pull my hair straight back and thereby look more like a Malay. For a few days I stayed mostly indoors and only ventured out when necessary.

But soon I was back at the chores and life became more interesting. Danger seemed to have receded and I was happy for the first time in many weeks. I gained weight and always felt hungry. My knowledge of the Malay language increased and I was able to answer the questions of the servants. The older servant was rather shy, but the younger one's inquisitiveness kept me busy providing suitable answers.

One particularly bright day I was feeling in exceptionally high spirits, and went about with a light heart doing the morning chores. At noon I bathed and after tidying up leaned out of the window to catch the gentle breeze. It was peaceful and it seemed impossible that a war could be going on. Yet I could not help thinking of the war and what it meant to me. Then I noticed a movement on the path and saw Chin Chye cycling towards me. This meant trouble and I bounded out of the house to meet him.

He smiled soberly when I asked, "What's the news?"

He eased his bicycle to the ground and motioned me to go inside the house. It was obvious that he didn't know where to begin.

"What is it, Chin Chye?" I asked.

"A high-ranking officer from Singapore has arrived," he said, looking at me intently, "and he'll be staying in Padang for a few days. They are looking for a girl to entertain him."

"But they don't want me?"

"They don't believe you are dead and there is a rumour that you are hiding in someone's house. MP Hashimoto has summoned the police and detectives and ordered them to find you. You have been described as wearing a frock, having short wavy hair and a bandaged leg. They even have your photo."

I remembered then that a Japanese soldier had taken a snapshot of us before we were interned and also that Susuki had taken one, though I found out later that Susuki had never revealed this fact.

Chin Chye continued, "Hashimoto has offered a reward of five guilders to anyone who gives information leading to your arrest, or whereabouts, dead or alive."

"So I am only worth five guilders, but I guess all Padang will be out searching for me."

"Pray to your God," he said, for he had no religion. "There is not much more we can do, Janet."

He said that the situation was getting increasingly dangerous and that I should improve my Malay disguise. On the following day his brother would bring me some more Malay clothes. I realised then that Chin Chye was quite right; now only God could deliver me from the Japanese. The hunt would be intensified and they would keep on searching until I was found.

It has always troubled me that I was never able to express the deep gratitude I felt for what the Oes and Keng Soon had done for me. Now I tried to convey my feelings by offering Chin Chye the gold cross and chain I always wore. I removed it and held it out to him saying, "Please take this and keep it as a symbol of our friendship. There is nothing I could say which would tell you how deeply grateful I am to the three of you. Please take this, my last and most treasured possession."

"Please keep it, Janet," he answered, embarrassed.

"No, I want you to have it. It may be the last time I'll ask you to do anything for me. You must go now."

He had no choice, so he took it and we walked back to his bicycle. We said goodbye and he assured me that everything would be all right. But nothing was all right, and the end was in sight. I watched him cycle away; never once did he turn back to look.

Ntjim was not well and stayed in bed. I went to her room and remained a few minutes with her. When I looked down on her pale thin face I felt that her days were numbered. The whole household was terrified at the news which Chin Chye had brought and I sensed that they wished I had never set foot in their house. I was sad and ashamed. I went to my room to be alone and to pray. When the little harelipped girl called me for dinner, I could not bring myself to face the family, nor was I hungry. I went into the backyard, and in walking around it I came upon a piece of rope. I pounced on it; here was the one thing that might spare me the shame I feared most, I could use this, if necessary, to end it all. I took it to the bathroom and wound it around my waist beneath my clothing before returning to my room. I then laid out the Malay costume and a bundle of false hair for the following day.

In the morning I dressed in the Malay clothes and pushed my hair straight back, and used the hair which had been given me and tied it all in a tight knot at the nape of my neck. As I looked into the mirror I was pleased with the disguise.

Suddenly the front door shook with thunderous knocking. One of the daughters rushed into the room and urged me to hide. There was fear in her voice; she was terrified. She told me that Malay policemen were surrounding the house. Quickly she helped to hide me under a bed. From where I lay I could hear Ntjim in the next room struggling out of bed to answer the door.

"What do you want?" she asked in Malay through the door.

"Where is *Nona* Singapore?"

"Go away. We do not know *Nona* Singapore."

"We will shoot every member of your family by order of the Kempetai Hashimoto if she is found in this house."

"She is not here and I dare you to shoot."

Her boldness temporarily convinced them. During the argument, the policemen at the back door left their post and moved to the front door so one of the daughters slipped into my room and whispered that the back entrance was now clear and told me to get going. Quickly I scrambled from my hiding place, slipped out of the door and ran for the mangrove swamps. I remember Ali, the errand boy, glaring at me as I hurried down the four steps.

I stumbled along in a panic and soon fell into a ditch. My sarong caught in some thorns and I had to struggle to get free. Again I ran on and fell knee-deep in mud. I looked at my leg. My old ulcer, covered with mud, trickled blood and pus. My hands had been scratched by the thorns and they too oozed blood. My sarong was torn and muddy and my bare feet throbbed with pain.

I scrambled across a narrow path and into a small clump of trees. Here it was dry and the earth was firm. I placed an arm around a trunk for support but as I rested, a movement among the dry leaves caused me to look up and I saw a huge snake slithering down towards me, its tongue darting in and out of its mouth. I made a desperate jump over a fallen log and ran on again until I found another large tree. There I slumped down.

Much later I heard a voice calling: "*Nona, Nona.*" It startled me and I hid behind the tree. When I recognised the voice I looked out and saw Ali carrying a basket. When he saw me he held it out. It contained my clothing.

He said that Ntjim did not want me to return to her house. It had been searched by the police shortly after my escape. When they failed to find me they swore they would get me that very day. Before Ali left he handed me ten guilders which had been found under my pillow.

Again I was alone, and very hungry and thirsty. I had eaten nothing since noon on the previous day. I looked through the basket of clothing hoping to find food but there was none. It was approaching midday and the blazing sun beat down. I realised that I was sitting at the edge of a clearing, so I crawled to a shadier spot. Above me the birds chirped and twittered and this only made me feel worse. I began to doubt whether God existed and wondered, if He did, why He had ever created me.

I began thinking up answers in case the police found me. I wondered whether it would be wise to be seen with the clothes and decided it was best to conceal them. I noticed that where I was sitting there was an abundant growth of *pucuk paku*, a kind of edible green fern which grows wild and looks like long nails. Many people in Padang used this vegetable for cooking and called them nail vegetables. I gathered enough to conceal the clothing in the basket.

I sprawled at the foot of the tree and tried to forget my miseries. I lay there for some time trying to rest. I dozed but was jerked back to my senses by the clanging of a bell. The noise stopped as I sat up but the silence was broken by the loud mooing of a cow. I thought that a small village might be nearby and that when night fell I might perhaps find shelter and food.

This comforting idea was short-lived for suddenly, out of nowhere, five men appeared. Each wore the armband of the Rising Sun.

One who held a notebook stared hard at me and asked in Malay, "What are you doing here?"

"I am resting," I replied.

They studied me carefully.

"What is your name?"

"Goh Lian Eng."

"Where do you live?"

"Compound China (Chinatown)."

"Are you married?"

"My husband died three years ago. I live by washing clothes."

They examined my basket and asked whose clothes they were. They talked in Dutch.

"Do you speak English?"

"No."

"Do you know Janet Lim?"

"No."

"Why do you come here to do your washing?"

"I did not come here to wash but to relieve myself and to take a rest."

"You are not Malay. Why do you dress like this?"

"The clothing is cool, and I can dress as I please."

One of them seized the hem of my sarong and drew it up to look at my legs. I tried to kick him but alas, he had seen my sore. After that they were sure they had found the person they were looking for.

The leader shouted and demanded to know why my sarong was torn and why I was covered with mud. And how had I got the sore? And why was I disguised? The whys and wheres came quickly and loudly. And I nodded and shook my head over and over again.

One of them produced two faded photographs and asked me to tell them who the people were. Although they were bad prints I recognised myself amongst a number of other internees.

"Tell me who these people are?" he shouted.

I shook my head. One of them grabbed my arm and pulled me to my feet. They ordered me to go with them and I had no alternative but to follow. One of them remarked that by my appearance it looked as though I had not eaten for days. We walked on in silence; I was terror-stricken and ashamed.

Finally we arrived at a shabby *atap* house. I was pushed up the stairs into a small room where I slumped into the chair that was offered me. Someone shouted to the owner of the house, "Bring rice."

When the owner came I was shocked. For I had seen him only a few days earlier at Ntjim's house. He had bought soap and I remembered that he had spoken to me. I glared at him and he roared with laughter. I was deeply humiliated. He put a plate of rice and a glass of water before me. I emptied the glass of water but pushed the rice aside. One of the men stood up and told me to thank my host for the water. But the host said, "Thank God for it."

Anger and hatred mounted within me and I stood up and shouted, "So you know God? If you fear Him, you would never sell me to the Japs. They will torture me and put me to death. My body will rest but my spirit will haunt you wherever you go."

I was seized by the wrist and yanked out of the room and down the stairs, where a carriage stood waiting. I was pushed into it and driven off. My five captors pedalled on bicycles beside the carriage, shouting happily to each other about their capture. The sun had already set and passing pedestrians stared curiously as the horse trotted slowly on.

Then suddenly with a jerk the horse came to a standstill. Someone shouted to me to get out. I staggered behind one of the men who led me through a large gate into a garden where I waited. Two Chinese approached me, one short and fat, the other tall and heavily set. They smiled at the sight of me. I saw women carrying babies in their arms, peeping through the windows, giggling and seemingly very much amused. One of my five captors addressed the tall man as Captain and then I knew I was in a well-known Chinese house. He rebuked me saying, "Why did you run away? You have put the Chinese in Padang into serious trouble."

"I ran away to save my own skin," I replied.

One of my captors shouted, "You said you did not speak English and you did not know a Janet Lim you liar!"

"Yes, I lied, but I am proud to say my parents would never have arrested a girl and sold her to the Japanese for five guilders. You could have helped me but you prefer to see me, a Chinese, become a prostitute. I ran away because I refused to be one. My skin is not as thick as yours. Yes, I am the Janet Lim—*Nona* Singapore—whom you are looking for."

The short man asked quietly, "What did the Japanese want you for?"

"They wanted to go to bed with me, do you understand?" I shouted at him.

Then I was ordered to get into his car and my basket of clothing was pushed in beside me. When my thoughts became clearer I regretted losing my temper and speaking so freely. As we drove past the market I realised that we were going to the Kempetai's office. The car came to a stop before it and we entered the gate. The place was swarming with

Japanese and I felt that I was doomed. I was taken to the reception room, which was crowded with people of all nationalities. I sat on the edge of a bench and waited. The man who had brought me to this place was called into a private office adjoining the reception room. I searched the sea of faces but none was familiar. The people in this room were in trouble like myself, therefore each was absorbed in his own thoughts and paid little attention to anyone else. In spite of the many people in it there was silence in the room; but angry voices could be heard coming from the private office and through the half-open door I saw two men stand up. The door was suddenly flung wide open and MP Hashimoto appeared glaring at me. The man who had brought me left by the side door. Then I was pushed violently into the office. There were many uniformed Japanese of various ranks. MP Hashimoto, who spoke through the interpreter, asked me why I had disguised myself in such a hideous way. The Kempetai made a swift motion with his hand and I braced myself to avoid the blow, but he reached to the back of my head for my knot of false hair and flung it on the floor with disgust. His subordinates laughed.

I wished the floor would open and swallow me. Hashimoto ordered me to change my clothes in their presence. It was not difficult to change from a sarong into a frock without being seen—it was a knack I had learnt at school. MP Hashimoto's interpreter, whose name I later learned was Kaneyama, was short and thin, and had a square face covered with small pockmarks. He could speak Hokkien and Malay fluently and knew a little English. He appeared to be as cruel as the Kempetai, if not worse. Then the questioning began.

"Where have you been since you left the hotel? With whom did you stay?"

"I did not stay with anybody. No one would shelter me. I have been in the jungle since I left the Yamato Hotel."

"Did you stay all this time—nearly three weeks—in the jungle?"

"Yes."

"Why did you run away from the hotel?"

"I ran away because I was disturbed nightly by Japanese soldiers trying to molest me. They wanted to treat me like a prostitute."

"You lie. No Japanese would do a thing like that. Why didn't you report this to me? You ran away without even paying your hotel bill. I have reasons to believe you are an American spy as well as a nurse. You work for the Americans, don't you? Tell me how many Americans and English there were on board the ship *Kuala*?"

I was surprised at this outburst. This was something new. Now I was a spy. He must be mad.

"I am not a spy. I know nothing about politics. I cannot tell you the number of Americans or English on the ship. I don't even know how many nurses there were on board. No, I am not a spy, please believe me. I don't know even one American."

Hashimoto pounded his fists violently on the table and his voice rose in anger.

"Do you realise what the Nipponese do to spies? We give them a slow death. The Nipponese people have been very kind to you but you have taken advantage of them. Who is your boss, and where is he now?"

The questioning continued without a break. Hashimoto's voice rose even higher; he banged the table and pointed his finger at me. My mind was so confused, that at one moment I was not sure whether I really were a spy or not—such was the effect of the Kempetai's grilling. I did not know how to answer. I was very thirsty and my mouth was parched. Kaneyama pushed me into a corner and whispered in the Hokkien dialect that if I spent the night with him he would help me. I became hysterical and cried, "You will have my dead body first, you dirty rat."

Hashimoto swung round to face us and he spoke something in

Japanese to Kaneyama and his face reddened. From a drawer in a small writing desk Hashimoto took out three revolvers and started looking them over. I watched him and felt myself growing cold and clammy.

But I felt that if I must die, I should be glad it would be by a bullet. I shut my eyes and thought of my adopted mother and of my friends who would never know what had happened to me. Hashimoto said something to Kaneyama who left the office. I bowed my head and said a prayer. I remained standing in front of Hashimoto who sat toying with his pistols. Minutes passed before Kaneyama returned. He spoke a few words to Hashimoto and left again. When he came back I had a shock, as Mao was with him. She was carrying my pillows and mat. She came forward quickly and said, "Hallo, my dear girl."

I did not answer her for her voice sounded unnatural. I was told they had given Mao all my belongings since I was going to die in a few minutes' time. Then the furious voice of MP Hashimoto began again, this time it was even fiercer than before. He shouted that he had given me time to tell him everything. He was adamant about the fact that I was a spy. His voice rang out as he paced up and down. Mao's mouth hung open. Kaneyama explained to her that because I was a spy Hashimoto was going to punish me. She was told, "Say goodbye now, your friend is going to die and you will never see her again."

I shall never forget the way Mao grabbed my things. Her hands busily gathered my clothes while she kept on saying, "Goodbye, my dear girl. God bless you. Do you want to leave a letter behind so that when the war is over I can deliver it?"

I was bewildered that she should be so empty of feeling. But I felt no bitterness towards her for after a few moments I would never see her again. She held my hand, then walked out of the office without looking back. Over and over the word spy rang out in my mind. To justify their action the Japanese would, after my execution, call me a dirty spy.

Hashimoto was again playing with his revolver and grinned when I stared at him. Suddenly I realised that I would be dead soon. Never again would I see my friends in Singapore or the Oe family, and I bit my lips to keep back my tears.

The men rose. Hashimoto took the three pistols and handed one to Kaneyama. I was ready to go. It was two in the morning; I had been questioned for eight hours. I touched Kaneyama's arm and said, "Please tell the Kempetai that I have a request. When I am dead, please say that I was a Chinese spy. I do not want to die for a country about which I know nothing."

I was taken out to a waiting car. The people of Padang had long since gone to bed, all was quiet and the night was dark. I stumbled and felt as if I were floating in air. I sat in the back of a car. Hashimoto drove with Kaneyama sitting beside him. We drove quite a distance and during that time I relived my life. Events of bygone days, happier days, flashed through my mind. When we slowed down, I heard the sound of dashing waves. I knew then that the execution was to take place on the beach—the usual Japanese method, which avoided the necessity of burying the body. I kept on telling myself to be brave. Hashimoto got out, followed by Kaneyama. As I stepped out Kaneyama caught hold of me thinking I was trying to escape. I laughed aloud and said, "Don't touch me, I won't run. I am more eager to die than you know."

A cool breeze blew gently but I shivered with cold, for over the tropical waves the night seemed ghostly and starless. The two Japanese pointed their pistols at me and ordered me to walk into the murky water. I stood still for a moment to make my last threat, "My spirit will haunt you when I die." As I stepped slowly into the cold water I repeated the Lord's prayer. When I was knee-deep I stopped. A mysterious indescribable sensation came over me when I felt so close to death. The waves dashed hard against my legs as I stood waiting. The minutes were long and I turned to see the two figures in the dark. Tears of self-pity rolled down my cheeks. I said my last prayer: "Please, Jesus, save my soul, and guard my friends in Padang and Singapore." Then I shouted, "I am ready!" and started counting one, two, three, to ease my mind. But the shots never came. I turned to face them again and once more shouted, "I am ready. Be quick."

Shutting my eyes I heard two shots and although I realised later they were not fired at me, I fainted. I must have fallen into the sea because when I regained my senses I was lying on the beach dripping wet. I heard words but they conveyed nothing. I was cold and my teeth chattered. "Where am I?" I wondered. I was brought back to earth when Hashimoto pulled me to my feet. He said something to Kaneyama who interpreted and said, "Say sorry."

"Why should I? I have done nothing wrong."

"You must apologise for running away and causing so much trouble to the Japanese people."

"You should apologise for hunting me." I was too late to avoid a blow which sent me spinning. Hashimoto came close to me and extended his hands in my direction with both thumbs up as he spoke. The interpreter explained that Hashimoto had been a member of the military police for twelve years in Japan and China, but he had only seen a few so bold and brave as I; for this reason he would not kill me now but would give me a slow death. I was shoved roughly into the car. What happened during that ride I cannot remember. All strength and feeling had gone out of me. The strain had left me limp; my senses were dulled. When we arrived back at the Kempetai's headquarters it was five in the morning. Someone seized me and half carried me across a path to a small cell, where I was sent flying to the ground. The door was closed, bolted and locked from the outside. In the darkness, I sat leaning against the concrete wall when suddenly I felt something stirring in the room.

Straining my ears I wondered if it might be the sentry posted outside. Then with my hand outstretched, I felt my surroundings and my blood seemed to freeze as I touched something warm. Slowly I made out the form of a man lying close to the opposite wall. His arms were spread out, his breathing slow and faint, and he seemed to be half dead. I thought he must have undergone extreme torture and been left in this cell to die. I neither moved nor spoke. A click and the door opened and the man was dragged out. The air was filled with cries of pain and agony. Somewhere close to me people were being tortured and their pleas for mercy were the last thing I remembered.

When next I opened my eyes I saw the shadows of bars cast upon the walls. The sun had already begun to add heat to the discomfort of the small cell; which was only about ten feet square. The walls and ceiling were concrete. The only means of ventilation: the iron-barred door.

A small dirty sink was fixed to the wall and a worn-out cord and bulb hung from the middle of the ceiling. The air was stuffy and smelly. A large kerosine tin stood in a corner for toilet purposes. Hashimoto's office was on my left and from my cell I could see the road and the reception room very well. The sentry at the door was a tall dark Malay with sharp features. He was curious to know why I was in the lockup and I was about to tell him when I saw a soldier hurrying across the path. He unlocked the door and stepped in with an air of authority. He pointed to the large tin and made signs that I was to carry and empty it. I was dismayed to see that it was half full. It was slippery, had no handle, and I had no strength to carry it. Slowly I shifted the tin across the cell and out on to the rough drive. As I dragged it over a bump the contents splashed the soldier's face. I laughed and he shouted furiously. We reached a drain, I emptied the tin into it, but I was too weak to pump water and wash it. On returning to my cell I slumped into a corner and wept bitterly. About an hour later a Japanese soldier brought a plate of rice and vegetable, and water. Although I had been without food for many hours I could only eat a mouthful. The horror of the previous night came back to me and I was seized with a fit of hysteria. My sobs grew louder and louder and I cried until the Malay sentry could not stand it. He begged me to stop and finish my food. Once again he asked why I was in the lockup. Between my sobs I told him of the pressure the Japanese had put on me to yield to their lust, and how I had been accused of being an American spy. He whispered that as far as he knew I was then the only girl in the prison.

Through the slowly moving day that kindly sentry spoke words of reassurance to me, but in the evening he was replaced by another Malay, a short, stocky man who was less sympathetic. He refused to let me face the door and each time I looked at the road, he pointed his rifle and threatened to shoot. He tormented me with insults and we quarrelled until he went off duty. Before sunset a Japanese soldier brought my straw mat and pillow which I had seen given to Mao. As I spread the mat on the floor, a man's face peeped through the bar. He was a Chinese sentry and looked very surprised when he saw me, but he waited until darkness came to question me about my capture. He suggested that I should escape with him, but he understood when I pointed out to him the obstacles which made his scheme impossible. He then offered to deliver a message to my friends in Padang. Although tempted, I dared not trust him. Across the path was the reception office and I could see the Japanese on duty, looking, every now and then, in my direction.

Early the next morning I heard shouts of "*Banzai!*" Japanese soldiers were lined up, bowing towards the rising sun. A few minutes later they marched past my cell; anger burnt within me and I shouted, "Shorty, you have no shame, stealing other people's countries," but no one took any notice of me. Soon afterwards a soldier unlocked my door and told me to perform my daily task of emptying the tin.

It was now much easier.

Some time that morning I had a shock when I recognised a familiar figure crossing the path near the office. It was with a sickly feeling that I saw Keng Soon enter the Kempetai's office. Why was he there? I was terrified that because of me he had got into trouble. He was in sight for only a few minutes and then disappeared.

Again I became absorbed in my own thoughts. "What shall I do?" An inner voice seemed to say: "God will help." But it also said: "No, there is no God, He was driven away by the sound of the bombs. What have I done that I should receive so much punishment? There is no God, no God!" I shouted between sobs.

Half an hour later MP Hashimoto and Kaneyama came to my cell. My eyes widened in horror at the sight of them. Hashimoto held out my gold chain and cross. I was alarmed for Keng Soon's safety. How had it fallen into the Kempetal's hands so quickly? It was only a few days ago that I had given it to Chin Chye.

"Where did you leave this chain?"

"In one of the cupboards at the hotel."

"You did not leave it in some other place?"

"No."

"Why did you take it off your neck?"

"It was my habit to take it off when I washed." Hashimoto handed the chain and cross to me and I was told to keep it and they left, smiling sarcastically. I was perplexed that it should be returned to me. Why did Keng Soon turn it over to the Kempetai? Later he told me that he used the chain and cross as an excuse to enter the Kempetai's office in order to try to find out what had happened to me.

Hashimoto's method of torture and the slow death he had promised were beginning to take effect. I could not sleep but paced the cell; my mind was in a turmoil. I quarrelled with the sentry and cursed the

197

Japanese. I was so filled with gloom and horror that I walked and talked to myself and yet I found no relief. The walls seemed to be closing in on me and I was afraid of being squeezed. Pressure mounted in my temples. The sun had gone down and I could bear it no longer. I cried, shouted, and damned the Japanese, at the same time I tore my hair and beat my chest. A Japanese soldier and the sentry rushed into my cell to restrain me. I cried long into the night. On the morning of the fourth day I refused to eat and lay on the ground, tossing and whining. The heat had become intolerable and I no longer felt human. I had been reduced to the existence of an animal and was not allowed to bath or to wash.

Hashimoto tormented me daily by appearing in my cell. I spat at him which seemed to delight him. The Chinese sentry got worried because I refused to eat. He brought a Japanese soldier with him. The sentry pleaded with me to eat and the soldier showed by signing that if I did not eat I would die. He said that no prisoners had ever refused food unless they were dying. Then he came back with a packet of ice-cream and two cakes and then disappeared. Later that evening another military policeman, junior in rank to Hashimoto, peered through the bars. He had seen me before and had shown a sympathetic attitude towards me. Now it was plain that he was shocked at my appearance. He glanced quickly right and left, and then tossed a small packet of sweets into the cell. He left as quickly as he came and I did not have time even to thank him. If any Japanese had been caught showing kindness to the prisoners, he would have been punished. So those who did so, did it surreptitiously.

Suddenly I remembered that I had a rope with me—this would be the way out. I waited for the sentry whom I disliked most to come on duty. I was unusually quiet and pretended to be asleep when he poked his rifle at me. The night was peaceful and quiet. Then I noticed that the guard was dozing off, nodding his head to left and right. Taking my rope from my waist I tied two knots, one on each side, so that they would fit exactly under the carotid arteries. Quickly and silently I tied the rope round my neck and drew it tighter and tighter. My head throbbed and whirled and seemed to grow bigger. My eyes bulged and tiny stars twinkled before them. As the stars grew fainter and fainter, darkness enveloped me and I lost consciousness.

When I looked up I saw a blurred figure and I was horrified to find it was a Japanese officer holding my hand. He must have found me just in time. He said something to me, but I could not make out what it was. Then I must have fallen off to sleep. When dawn broke I was too exhausted either to move or to sit up, my body ached and my neck and chest were so painful that it was agony to stir. My limp body was stretched on the floor and the blazing sun added its cruelty. The foul-smelling cell increased my misery. I started yelling but my voice had become very weak. A Japanese soldier thrust a thermometer into my mouth and soon returned with six quinine tablets which I swallowed. Then I dreamt of my real mother. She came towards me with outstretched arms and told me that she had been looking for me. She said that she was going to cook me my favourite dish. In my dream I said: "Mama, you must not leave me again, I am very lonely and everybody hates me." But to my dismay she began to recede, growing smaller and smaller until her face became so blurred that I could see her no longer. "Mama, do not leave me, please," my voice rang out. I got on to my feet and staggered round the cell. The Malay guard was furious; he pointed his rifle and called out, "*Perempuan gila* [mad woman]." Soon this guard was replaced by the Chinese man, who produced a bottle of water and told me that the Americans had bombed Singapore. "Who cares?" I thought. I was no longer interested and only hoped for death.

I had lost count of the days I had spent in the cell. One evening a bearded man in Japanese uniform brought in my evening meal. Looking at me he told me to eat up my food and get up some strength.

"Stop crying and do not worry. We will send for help; I am a Chinese." I was too stunned to answer, and by the time I had realised the implications of what he had said he had disappeared. The following morning I was jolted to my feet and I staggered behind a Japanese soldier who signed to me to follow him. Outside my prison gate stood Tomtit. He looked surprised at seeing me and asked how long I had been in the cell, but I could only shake my head. Then he spoke again, but I did not understand his Chinese, so our conversation came to a dead end. Roughly I was pushed back into my cell and the heavy door was bolted from the outside.

It was on a Sunday (28 June, I think) after I had been a week or so in the cell, that the door was finally thrown wide open. A Japanese soldier came in followed by a Malay. Aimlessly I staggered behind them. The Malay handed me over to a woman who took me to a bathroom and told me to wash myself. Since I had been captured I had not had a wash and I had almost forgotten how to wash. My dress was very dirty, torn and smelly, my matted hair fell untidily about my face and I must have looked more like an animal than a human being. I was taken to the office, in which I had been questioned, but all feeling had gone from me, so that I stood in front of MP Hashimoto without hatred or emotion. After waiting a few minutes, Hashimoto Tada appeared. One look at me and he muttered words of regret. I was then told that I was free—free to live with my friends. MP Hashimoto said that he was even willing to give me the permit which he had refused me before.

"I am your prisoner," I replied, " do what you like. I have lost the will to live; besides, nobody in Padang would have me. They are afraid of me because I have been under the Kempetai. I hate you Japanese because you have broken my spirit."

Hashimoto Tada said, "The Nipponese do have a bad name because a few like you have been treated roughly, and these stories have spread and now everybody says that we are bad. Am I very bad?" he asked, smiling.

Later he told me that as soon as he had heard of my escape he had given instructions that he was to be told if they captured me. He knew that if I was sent to the Kempetai headquarters I would suffer severely. He had only heard a few days before about my capture.

"Why did you bother so much about me?" I asked him.

"Because when I lived in Singapore I was treated very well by the Chinese."

A little later to my great surprise Mao arrived. Once again I heard her familiar greeting, "Hallo, my dear girl, how are you?"

"I am very well, as you can see," I laughed aloud.

Poor Mao, she had been pushed from pillar to post because of me. Hashimoto Tada told Mao to take me out for a walk and to return to the office before 4 p.m. as they were looking for a place for me to stay.

I was too weak to walk properly, but supported by Mao I staggered outside the gate. The only people I wanted to see were the Oes. After a short distance I rested on a stone outside the Roman Catholic Church, which faced the Convent School. I casually watched the people entering the church. Anger and hatred rose within me when I saw a familiar figure—the Chinese who had captured and sold me for five guilders. "Look, he is going to church," I shouted. "How can he do such a thing? Did he stop to think of what I would have to suffer when he captured me and handed me over to the Kempetai? Look, he is making the sign of the Cross," I shouted again.

I vowed that as long as I lived I would never enter another church. I hated God and all men and most of all I hated myself.

I am not surprised now that my faith fell to pieces at that time. Most of my belief had been learnt in the Mission School, which I had left at the age of sixteen and a half. I had been taught a simple faith in Christ as my Lord and Saviour, and the necessity for Christian behaviour, especially kindness and integrity in daily work. As I have described earlier, my religious experiences at the Mission Hospital were unfortunate, and then later the suffering and mental strain I had endured damped out the little light I had. Except for the two moments when I was in danger, on the raft and on the beach waiting to be shot, when God had seemed very close to me, He seemed to have gone out of my life. It took me a long time to find Him again.

When we finally arrived at the Yamato Hotel I was physically and mentally exhausted. Keng Soon was alone in the office and he was surprised to see us. As Mao was with me I had to pretend that I had come to pay my hotel bill. I was afraid that she might tell the Japanese unintentionally that the Oes had helped me all along. When we were having tea, Tjin Hoe joined us. He had just returned from church and told me that he had met my captor.

"Yes, Tjin Hoe, I saw him and I have made up my mind not to have anything to do with the Christians again."

"Oh, Janet, do not say such a thing. You must forgive and forget. Perhaps he was under orders to arrest you and he had to do his duty."

When Mao was out of earshot I said, "I want to thank you, your brother and Keng Soon, for all you have done for me. No words can express how grateful I am and I shall not forget you all as long as I live. Goodbye, I must go."

"Where are you going?"

"I do not know, I do not care."

Broken in spirit and my faith gone, accompanied by Mao, I walked towards the hotel gate, Tjin Hoe and Keng Soon looking after us with worried expressions.

Nursing Again
July 1942–August 1944

Mao and I arrived at MP Hashimoto's office at four o'clock as we had been ordered to do. A car was waiting for us in which were another Japanese officer named Inou and Hashimoto Tada, and we drove away in silence. The car stopped in front of a simple Malay house and we were ushered up the few steps into a sitting room. No sooner were we in our seats than another large car stopped in front of the house. Its occupants were well-known Chinese residents in Padang. They were the people to whose house my captors had taken me when they caught me. They greeted the two Japanese officers, but eyed me coldly. Finally one of them said, "You are going to stay at the president's [Tomtit's] house."

"Are you prepared to guarantee my safety?"

"How ungrateful you are! Don't you trust these gentlemen who have been so good to you?"

"I do not trust any men, especially men like you, with your sweet talk."

They left soon, but Hashimoto Tada and Inou remained with us till late in the evening. The latter kept on singing Chinese songs.

My hostess, a kind and sympathetic elderly Malay woman, lived in this house with her two daughters. I never discovered her name. She and her daughters offered us cakes and drinks but did not press me to talk. Arrangements had been made for me to remain with them for the night.

The woman brought me some Malay medicated oil and rubbed my body with it. Looking at my swollen chest and sore neck, she asked, "The Japanese did this to you?"

"No, I did it myself because I wanted to die."

I was attended on by all the women in the house, Mao combing my matted hair while the two young girls massaged my legs. I relaxed on the comfortable bed and soft pillows and soon fell into an exhausted sleep. I was awakened by a hearty shake and a voice calling, "*Nona, Nona*." I could not remember where I was until I saw Mao. She helped me to dress. Towards the evening Hashimoto Tada and Inou came and told Mao to pack my belongings for we were to leave the house. Mao's mouth hung wide open.

"Me too?" she asked.

"Yes, you are going to keep your friend company."

She looked vacantly at me, and I thought that she must have wished she had never met me. We thanked our hostess and reluctantly followed the men to the waiting car which took us to a very large and attractive house. The vast garden was alive with flowers and trees. The house was divided into blocks; in the centre one lived the president, the left block was partly occupied and on the right was a row of rooms for the servants. A small path led through the garden to the house of Wakamatsu and Hashimoto Tada. The place was well guarded by Malay sentries. We were greeted by an old Japanese named Ada who came from Penang and kept house for the president. The latter was waiting to interview us. Sitting round the table, besides Tomtit, were Wakamatsu and a Japanese officer, and the four of us joined them. I pointed a finger at Wakamatsu and said, "He is the only man with a heart."

The president wanted to know what I was saying. Wakamatsu's face flushed and he told him about the incident at Yamato Hotel. The president nodded his head. They talked for a long time in Japanese. Later I was told that the president warned them to treat me with the utmost kindness, seeing that this was the only thing which could bring me back to normal.

The housekeeper, Ada, took me round the house and asked me to choose a vacant bedroom but I refused to do so although the rooms were beautiful. I told him that they were too grand for me, and after my experiences in the rooms of the Yamato Hotel, I thought to myself that they were too dangerous. Finally, he took me to the servants' quarters where I chose a room between the cook's and Mao's. All the servants wanted to know who we were and where we had come from, and we were asked endless questions. As the main buildings were always full of Japanese, Wakamatsu thought it would be safer to block up the side entrance to the servants' quarters so that no one could enter except by the main door; this latter was kept locked and the cook was made responsible for the key. I often heard Wakamatsu tell the cook to help us and to feed us well, but I could not eat. I was very depressed and for days I sat without uttering a word. Later I was told that Mao had to teach me everything, even how to take a bath.

After several weeks in this depressed state I remember that one evening Mao and I went out in the garden. Everything was quiet and peaceful, until two Japanese arrived leading a large horse. One of them was learning to ride. He was very fat and short and no sooner was he in the saddle than he was thrown off and his feet caught in the stirrup and he was dragged along the path. His stomach bounced up and down. It was a most amusing sight, which made me laugh, a thing I had not done for weeks. Wakamatsu and Hashimoto Tada had been watching. They approached us, but I did not shrink from them as usual.

Later I was asked if I would help to arrange flowers and lay the table in the president's house. I was glad to have something to do, so these became my daily tasks. On a very hot morning when I had just finished cutting flowers Mao helped me to carry the vases to the house. We came face to face with the president. He had not a stitch on. Shocked, we dropped our vases and took to our heels. I was very angry with the cook for not telling us that the president was ill and had not gone to his office, because as long as there were any Japanese in the house I would never go into it. The cook told me that the president often walked about the house naked and advised me not to worry. My daily tasks increased from arranging flowers to serving meals and making tea. I had become a housemaid without pay.

One night the president entertained all the military police. I was in the kitchen when the guests began to arrive. Amongst them was MP Hashimoto who shouted, "Hey, China!" and came towards the kitchen. Wakamatsu quickly grasped the situation and hurried to my side advising me to go to my room. He said, "Miss Lim, in future if there are guests in the house, please stay in your room. If an important guest asked for you, it would be very awkward for us to refuse him."

I was very grateful to him and he became my friend. One day he asked about my parents and I told him how I had become a slave, and how I was rescued and brought up by missionaries.

"Do you mean to say that the white people can be so kind?"

"Yes, especially the ones at my school." I then showed him Miss Kilgour's faded photograph which I had saved from the sea.

He looked at the photograph and said, "I would not have thought that white people could be so good. I have never come into contact with any Europeans, so I do not know them, but at my training school we were told..." He stopped abruptly in the middle of the sentence. Then changing the subject, he showed me a photograph of a very pretty Japanese girl. "This is the girl I was engaged to, but before I left home I broke off the engagement."

"Why?"

"Because I do not know how long the war is going to last; I might get killed and it is not fair to ask her to wait for me."

"Where is she now?"

"I do not know."

"You do not write to her?"

"No, a Japanese soldier believes that he should not let women interfere with his duty."

In the middle of our conversation Hashimoto Tada joined us and I retreated hurriedly, but Wakamatsu said, "Hashimoto Tada is my very good friend; why do you hate him so much? He has always wanted to help you."

"Mr Wakamatsu, I do not like working in the house, especially serving at tables when there are Japanese guests. Could you please find me another job?"

Soon, however, Mao and I were given a new job—sewing flags. We worked in a place only a few minutes away from our quarters. It was a house occupied by six Japanese whom we seldom saw as they went to work early. We worked from nine to half past twelve and two until five. There were two electric sewing machines and we turned out many Rising Suns daily, to the accompaniment of a lot of chatter with the servants of the house. One morning on my way to work I met one of my captors who smiled and said, "Is it not better to be a Japanese keep than to be wandering about? Look how happy you are now."

I was so angry that I spat at him!

Some of the local people undoubtedly thought that I was a mistress of the Japanese. My struggles with the Japanese Kempetai had made the Chinese very cautious about associating with me for they felt that at any moment they also might become involved. Besides this, they knew that I had been taken from the internment camp to the Yamato Hotel and in their eyes that could only mean one thing. To make it worse they saw me coming out daily from the president's house—and again drew the inevitable conclusion. It was impossible to escape from this round of accusations—a Japanese spy, an Allied spy, a collaborator, a mistress. As a result I found it best to avoid the local people; so, except for the Oes, I had no friends. Anyway it did not make any difference to me then what the people thought of me as I cared little for their opinion.

Soon after this Mao became restless and depressed. I realised that she thought I was directly responsible for her troubles, and certainly it was because of me that she had been dragged to so many places.

"I am sorry, Mao, but if you have a place to go to, please ask Hashimoto Tada, I am sure he will let you go."

She wasted no time but haunted his house by day and by night. One evening she rushed in rather excited, and told me in a happy voice that she was leaving me. I learned that she was to become the fifth wife of the old jeweller who tried to make me his fourth wife at the Yamato Hotel.

"Goodbye and good luck to you, Mao." We shook hands and never met again.

One evening Hashimoto Tada told me that he was going to take over the Indareong Cement Factory which was about ten miles outside Padang. There was a clinic there, run by a Malay who knew nothing about nursing. Hashimoto Tada thought that it would be an ideal job for me there, one in which I could earn a living. I thought at once of my Indian friend, who was a nurse.

"Hashimoto-san, may I ask a favour? I have a friend in the internment camp and I would be very grateful if she could come and work with me. I shall be lonely there by myself."

"You will have to ask Wakamatsu-san for that," he answered.

I pleaded with Wakamatsu, who neither promised nor refused. Daily

I pestered him. "Surely you are not going to send me to look after several thousand coolies by myself. Please let my friend Lily out."

Then one evening I received the happy news that she was coming; it excited me so much that I was unable to sleep. I went to work as usual but my eyes watched the road for Wakamatsu's car. When it arrived I was very disappointed to see my friend burying her head in her hands, She looked up when the car pulled up, and when she saw me she stopped crying.

"Oh, Janet! Janet! If only I had known that I was joining you, I would not have wept."

"Do you mean that Wakamatsu did not tell you?"

"Well, when I was in the office signing some papers, he muttered something about me working with Chiu Mei, but I had no idea who she was."

She told me that the internees were very angry with Wakamatsu for taking her away and had made a great row. Since Mao and I had been removed, the internees had demanded an order to the effect that no Japanese should take any woman away. She said that after I had escaped from the hotel the Japanese had searched the camp many times.

"Oh, Janet, how wonderful to feel this comfortable chair. I can hardly believe my eyes. Are these things real?"

I thought of the thousands of internees in Padang and was sad to see Lily feeling the furniture.

"This is a beautiful house, Janet."

"I am not staying here. It belongs to six Japanese. It is my workshop. I think we had better leave now because they will come back soon."

On our way to my room in the servants' quarters, Lily told me that life in the camp was getting worse every day. We talked about the job we were going to do in Indareong.

"Do you think it is safe for us to go, Janet?"

"I think their promises are genuine this time."

The following day we visited Indareong Cement Factory. The clinic was very small and stood in one corner of the estate near a rubbish dump. The place was smelly, full of flies, and dirt and dying dogs surrounded the small stairway leading up to the door of the clinic. The Malay in charge showed us a few rusty instruments and told us there were hardly any drugs or equipment. We consulted Hashimoto Tada; we told him the clinic was too small to cater for the two thousand or so Malay and Chinese coolies and their families. Despite the conditions in the clinic, we were very pleased with our visit and on the way back to Padang we decided that we would like the work.

On 27 July 1942, we left the president's house for the factory. It was the first time I felt that I was really free, and with a light heart I climbed into the waiting car. Curious people stared at us, and when Hashimoto Tada, who was driving, stopped to buy a box of matches, someone whispered: "Look, there is *Nona* Singapore! Fancy, she is now going about with the Japanese. I wonder who the other girl with her is."

I was very sad to hear these remarks, and Lily told me that even some of the internees in the camp had said that I was living with the Japanese. But she comforted me by saying, "I believe you have won the fight, so do not worry about what people think." Lily was always wise and full of good advice, although she was only a few years older than me.

We were amazed when Hashimoto Tada unlocked the door of a lovely house. Apparently, our complaints about the dirt of the old clinic had had some effect. "The clinic is there," he pointed to another house about a stone's throw away. After he had left us to inspect the factory, we wasted no time going through our residence. It had three bedrooms with surrounding verandahs, a dining room next to the kitchen and a large comfortable sitting room from which we could see the clinic and the office of the factory. Our verandah at the back looked upon a deep stream which ran down from the hills around Indareong.

After we had tidied the house up, we began to clean up the clinic. Next to it were two houses, one vacant, the other occupied by a Chinese family, who eyed us curiously and were rather cautious about making friends with us. The vacant house attracted my attention, as a thin wild-looking dog stood guarding its door. I learned later that the occupants had been taken away by night and when morning came the dog had looked sad and puzzled. It had been his habit to wait for his master at a certain hour of the day, and when the master failed to turn up for weeks on end, he began to howl. I tried to feed him, but he snapped at me.

Before Hashimoto Tada left us, we handed him a list of the equipment and drugs which we needed for the clinic. He arranged for a Malay to be our assistant. We were supposed to treat all minor cases and to visit families who could not come to the clinic. Only those with whom we could not cope were to be sent to Padang Hospital. We were to be on call alternately at night.

At last the clinic was ready and a red cross was painted on its roof for safety. The day the clinic was opened we received an endless stream of patients. Most of them were suffering from yaws, dirty ulcers and boils. We were amazed at their appearance—they wore only rags hanging from their waists, their torsos were usually bare and their faces were covered with cement. Besides dressing their wounds, we tried to teach them personal hygiene, but it was a hopeless task. Soon we received complaints; too many coolies attended the clinic and no work was being done in the factory! They were very curious to see who we were and what we looked like. Some said we were Japanese, others that we were spies employed by the Japanese; all were cautious and rather distant and we found it difficult to make friends with them.

We found we could not do a full day's work at the clinic, cook our own meals and do odd jobs outside, so we decided to employ a servant. Someone from the office recommended a Malay woman. We asked to see her. Lily and I were in our sitting room when she arrived. She almost crawled on all fours and when she was in the room she knelt facing us, her hands touching the floor. I told her to sit on a chair, but she looked at me as though I were mad. After we had agreed to engage her, she left us by retreating to the door in the same way as she had come in. I ran after her to observe her more closely, thinking she might be deformed and was surprised when I saw her walking away quite normally. I had never had a servant before and this grovelling attitude worried me. When this woman started work, she continued to crawl about the house, and this annoyed me so much that I decided to get rid of her. Later we found out that all the servants in this region were obliged to bend down when speaking to their mistresses and to retreat backwards when leaving the room.

One day we had four visitors, a Malay with a Japanese wife, whom he had married before the war, and two Japanese officers. Though uninvited, they made themselves at home and one of them called us from the clinic. As we entered our sitting room, the Malay asked us to serve tea because they were important visitors.

"Sorry, but we have only water in this house. We have not received our salary yet."

The Malay and his Japanese wife were angry with us and asked us to explain why we had been given such a lovely house.

"You are British running dogs and should be in an internment camp," shouted the Japanese woman.

She wanted to remove all the furniture from the house, but I told her to ask Hashimoto Tada before she took any such action. Meanwhile the two Japanese officers, who did not speak Malay, looked rather bored and finally persuaded the couple to go.

The following evening Wakamatsu and Hashimoto Tada paid their first visit. We told them of the incident.

"Do not worry about that couple, they are mad. That woman was interned by the Dutch; she is a nobody but because the Japanese have won the war, she thinks she has become very important," said Hashimoto Tada.

"But the war is not over yet."

"Soon we will have Australia—Australia very big."

"Surely the Australians will fight?"

"Remember how easily we took Singapore; though the British had more troops than we had."

"Hashimoto-san, I thought you said you were a civilian in Singapore?"

"Yes, I went into hiding and the stupid English never arrested me. When the Japanese landed in Singapore I joined them."

It was now clear to me that Hashimoto Tada had been a spy before the war.

We were delighted when at the end of the month we received our salary of seventy guilders each from the factory. Out of this we paid two and a half guilders income tax.

One day Hashimoto Tada told us that Wakamatsu was on his way to Singapore and that if we wanted to send any messages he would take them for us. Since we had left on 13 February we had had no news of our people. Hurriedly we each scribbled a letter and took them personally to Padang. It was agony waiting for news.

"Do you think my husband is alive, Janet? I had been married only three days when I left him. Do you think he has taken another woman?"

"I should not worry if I were you; the father of one of my friends had sixteen wives." I winked at her.

When he returned Wakamatsu brought us splendid news—our people were alive! With trembling hands and eyes full of tears we read and re-read our letters. Mine was from my classmate; my adopted mother had moved to another place.

These letters made us homesick. Wakamatsu was going again to Singapore, but he could not take us with him as he was flying. I gave him fifty dollars to give to my adopted mother. He advised us to ask Hashimoto Tada's permission to leave, for he was responsible for us.

Soon we were told that a Japanese from Pekanbaru was visiting Padang and would help us to get home safely. Most of our time until we left was devoted to shopping, for we heard that people in Singapore were starving.

The president signed all the travel documents and on 22 September 1942 we left for Padang. There we were introduced to our Japanese host and went on with him by car. The road was extremely rough, and though the scenery was magnificent I was too carsick to enjoy it. We arrived at Pekanbaru at 2 a.m. and were housed with a Malay couple. Next morning our Japanese host sent his car to fetch us. On the way from Padang he had not spoken more than two words with us, but now he insisted on our joining him in the prayers he said before breakfast. Later he put his car and chauffeur at our disposal while he attended to his business. Lily said, "I don't understand why some of the Japanese are so good to us while others are ready to cut off our heads."

We stayed several days at Pekanbaru, and haunted the waterfront waiting for a boat. Our host was very kind to us. One morning at prayers he said, "O God, I pray thee to keep all prisoners happy until peace is restored. Bless these two girls and guard them until they reach their homes and loved ones. Amen." He was a Methodist and had helped in his little church in Japan until he was called up. His eldest son had been killed by a bomb, and he showed us a photograph of his family, and said, "War no good." His actions and prayers set me thinking again. Here was a man—my enemy—praying for me. His son had been killed, yet he showed no bitterness. "Love your enemies." Here I saw this being lived. Some of us had strayed far from standards such as these. I was very ashamed of myself. I remembered incidents in my home in China. Once I was playing with a boy who threw a knife at me. My father bandaged me without making any fuss and that same evening he took the boy out for a walk. When I asked him for an explanation, he said, "Jesus loves everybody, Chiu Mei." That night before I went to bed I prayed, which I had not done for a long time.

At last we embarked on a small cargo boat. As we neared Singapore we stood on deck looking at it, and we remembered how, seven months before, it had been a ball of fire. Now its once proud harbour looked like a graveyard with the skeletons of ships lying half-submerged. When the boat pulled alongside, Lily and I said goodbye to each other. I hired a small van which took me through the quiet streets. As I neared my home I noticed a small boy running and shouting, "Auntie Chen, your daughter is home." My adopted mother ran out of her kitchen and stared at me as though I were a ghost. Then, with tears streaming down her cheeks, she cried, "Is that you, Janet?" Soon I was surrounded by my friends and my adopted family and we talked late into the night. My adopted mother told me what had happened after I left Singapore.

"When you did not come home after the British had surrendered I sent the two boys and a friend to the military hospital to search for you. They were shocked to find the hospital in ashes. They wandered about among the ruins, when a Malay appeared and told them that the Japanese were killing any Chinese they found. So they came home quickly and, as it became known that the Japanese were slaughtering the Chinese in thousands, I hid them in an attic, only letting them come down for baths. Later, I became convinced that you were dead."

215

Next morning I set out to visit my friends. On the way I passed a British prisoner-of-war camp; although the men looked exhausted, they were singing as they cleaned the drains and loaded trucks. My friends were delighted to see me, but seemed cautious. They told me to be careful and said, "Even your best friends can betray you." A few days later I met the Reverend Sorby Adams who had not yet been interned. He, with the Bishop of Singapore and one other priest, was allowed to continue pastoral duties for fifteen months after the surrender. On my way home I saw a Japanese soldier pulling the hair of a Chinese woman. She screamed for help and the Japanese kicked her; people in the road took no notice. Padang was peaceful compared with Singapore.

Soon I became restless and doubted the wisdom of my return. It was essential that I should work. Armed with the recommendation of the President of Padang I went out job-hunting. At the Kandang Kerbau Hospital I was told to report for duty as soon as possible; as a senior nurse I was to be paid forty dollars a month, with board and lodging provided. The hospital had suffered considerably from artillery and air-raids. All races were treated but the Japanese were put in the first-class wards. There were only three Japanese nurses; one of them could speak many Malayan languages but the matron could not speak a word of Malay, Chinese or English. She was rather moody and the duty rosters were disorganised, so that we never seemed to know what our duties were. The food was poor and we used to eat outside the hospital when we could. I was detailed to a third-class ward containing a hundred beds. The Malayan doctors and nurses with whom I worked were very pleasant indeed. But we never uttered a word about the war for we were all suspicious of each other. As the months went by cotton wool, gauze and lint became very scarce; the used materials were washed and sterilised many times.

The Japanese encouraged the use of their language and a class was started for which 150 people entered. Those who had had a Chinese education found it easy, but for me it was difficult. There were, however, many advantages to knowing the official language: it reduced the occasions when one was shouted at and humiliated, and it made one able to handle the Japanese more effectively. I found that before long I knew enough for simple conversation.

On 15 February 1943 the Japanese celebrated the first anniversary of the fall of Singapore. All nurses had to take part in the celebrations, which included a visit to the Japanese shrine, Rai Toa Gekijo, on a hill in the centre of the island, and a parade in the Jalan Besar Stadium. A truck took me with several other nurses to the top of the hill. A long wooden pole with Japanese writing on it had been placed there and behind it stood a wooden cross. These were to commemorate the Japanese and British who had died fighting in the area. Yamashita, the "tiger of Malaya", who had led his army over this hill, was not forgotten. We were told to face the wooden pole and bow three times, and after this to pay homage to the wooden cross. While we were doing this, a photograph was taken and, to our surprise, it appeared in the local press with the caption: "Japanese nurses paying respect to British soldiers who died during the campaign."

One afternoon I was summoned with four other nurses to the Medical Officer's office. The Medical Officer said, "I am sorry, I have unpleasant news for you. I have received orders that you should be paid twenty dollars a month instead of forty and that you should refund the money you have drawn in excess of this since you joined the hospital. You can take time to decide whether you want to continue in the service of the hospital or to resign." We were stunned. Out of my salary I gave twenty dollars to my adopted mother and only just managed to live on the rest. I wrote my letter of resignation at once. My adopted mother was very worried and said, "You cannot walk out of Japanese employment. Although the British have a colour bar, they have laws; the Japanese punish according to their moods." I began to wonder what would happen.

"Mama, today is Sunday and I am going to church. God will help me."

"It is good that you have faith. I am beginning to wonder where God is."

"Mama, you must not say that. God is always there."

Three days later I received a letter from the hospital, unsigned but with a Japanese imprint. It ordered me to return to duty or to refund the money, threatening further action if I did not. I dared not tell anyone about it. Just then I heard of a Japanese patient who wanted a private nurse. I packed my bag.

After a week I went home and found another letter from the hospital; as I was opening it, there was a knock at the door and there stood Hashimoto Tada. I did not tell him my troubles, but asked him if I could go back to the cement factory. He said, "Of course, you should have come back earlier. Singapore is such an expensive and crowded place." He told me to write to the authorities at the factory and promised to negotiate with them. After several weeks, during which I did private nursing, I heard that I could go back to Indareong. Simultaneously a third threatening letter arrived; as I was on the point of leaving I readdressed it to the hospital. Today I suspect that these unsigned letters were not sent by the Japanese authorities but by someone who wanted to cause me trouble. But I also see now that I ran a great risk in leaving Singapore in this way, for I might well have been followed by the Kempetai and so might my adopted family. My main reason for going back to Indareong was not that conditions were easier there but that the underlying fear and mistrust in Singapore were terrible. One never knew who was an enemy and who a friend. Very few people knew of my departure.

I embarked on the *Kikumaru*, a steamship carrying about twenty passengers. By luck a Japanese was going to inspect the factory and was able to give me a lift from Pekanbaru. A representative from the factory welcomed him at Pekanbaru and a large car from the factory awaited him. After almost bowing their heads off they very nearly drove away without me, but the driver reminded them. We followed the same road we had used on the way to Singapore and again I was carsick.

Not long after my return a Chinese girl, Doris Lim, who was a survivor of a shipwreck during the evacuation from Singapore, came to help me in the clinic. Together we did what we could for the health of the villagers but so many of their customs were most unhygienic.

In our times off duty we tried to help the community in other ways. I was asked if I could teach the Chinese children their language. I only knew about a hundred Chinese characters and told them that it was therefore impossible for me to become a teacher of Chinese. Before the war I had taught in Sunday School and also had taught the Brownies in Singapore, but I felt that a Chinese class was beyond me. However, the Chinese residents pestered me to try, so I gave way and started with a class of twenty-four pupils ranging from six to fourteen years of age. I was paid with three pounds of rice and one pound of sugar a month. We began with a Japanese song; this was compulsory. Unfortunately my Chinese class lasted for only a few months because, when I had finished teaching them what I knew, I had nothing more to contribute to their knowledge.

At this time I was not at all well. One doctor said that I was suffering from general weakness, another that I had contracted tuberculosis. Both agreed that I needed a complete rest and the Japanese were most generous in allowing me to stop work for two months while continuing to pay me the usual salary. Twice a week I went to Padang

219

for vitamin injections. After two months an X-ray was taken of my lungs and it was found that I was clear of tuberculosis; this greatly relieved my mind. I had put on some weight, so I went back to work and for the next twelve months life moved on in comparative calm.

In 1944 tension increased in Indareong. Many more Japanese had come and there was much military activity. AA guns had sprung up on all sides and soldiers guarded the factory. The Japanese believed that the Americans would attack the factory and said that it was the only undamaged one in Japanese-occupied territory. Wakamatsu, whom I had not seen for a long time, came to see me, as he was going away soon. When we started talking about the war he looked uneasy.

"Wakamatsu-san, do you now admit that you are losing the war?"

"No, you are wrong."

"We are friends and therefore I dare to speak to you like this. A year ago there were hardly any troops in Indareong; now the place is swarming with soldiers. You are expecting bombing, aren't you? Please tell me because I do not want to be killed by the Americans."

"You must be a spy since you seem to know so much."

"I wish I were; a spy is always a clever person." He changed the subject.

"I am leaving tomorrow and I hope to be able to send you a postcard. By the way, how much Japanese can you understand?"

"If you write in katakana, I can understand."

He told me that if he were captured he would commit hara-kiri. He said, "If I am captured by the enemy it will be a disgrace to my family. The British and the Americans when they are released feel happy because they are welcomed at home and their country will honour them, but we suffer shame when we face our families again."

I received a postcard from him after he had arrived at Bukit Tinggi and later I heard that he was interned somewhere near Singapore.

Whether he ever committed hara-kiri, I do not know.

In August 1944 I was talking to Morita-san, the head of the factory. He said, "There will be an exercise at Bukit Tinggi tomorrow and you will see a lot of planes; some may even fly over Indareong."

He smiled proudly as he spoke of his country's air force.

War Comes and Goes

August 1944–September 1945

A group of Japanese stood in front of the factory gazing intently towards the sky. Smiling, one said:

"Lim-san, look at our beautiful planes."

"Where?"

"There," he pointed.

I excused myself and hurried to our house. I felt uneasy; for by this time I knew the shape and sound of Japanese planes and I was sure that those I had seen and heard were not Japanese. Yet I dared not enter an air-raid trench for if they turned out to be Allied planes I should be accused of being a spy with prior knowledge of their movements. Hurriedly I changed and shouted to our servant to get breakfast ready for me. I was tying my shoelace when the first bomb dropped. I dived into the air-raid trench and our servant fell in on top of me. Many planes flew past and dust and cement swept over us in a hurricane. Then I heard someone shouting, "*Nona* Janet." It was my neighbour's daughter. Her mother and her youngest sister had gone to the market and her father was away. I summoned what little courage I had left and dashed across the road to the house. The eldest daughter aged twelve was cooking, the second child was having her bath and the third child, a boy of five, was still in bed. I dragged the whole lot to the trench. The bombing lasted for about ten minutes, then there was an interval and it started again.

When I thought that it was safe to get out I found that I was covered in mud. Dazed, I staggered towards the clinic and prepared to receive the casualties which I knew would soon pour in. Then I heard Doris calling:

"Janet, are you alive? Where are you?"

"Oh, Doris, thank God you are safe."

There was no time for further comment for the first casualties were arriving. All the office staff offered to help us. Every inch of the floor was taken up and we had to spread the wounded far outside the clinic. There were not enough drugs but we did our best; the dead were separated from the living. Later, two military doctors, drugs and an ambulance arrived from Padang and those patients who had any hope of recovery were transferred there. About sixty were very seriously wounded; in addition, many had been killed and a few buried alive. All the casualties were Malay or Chinese coolies except for two Japanese civilians and two Japanese soldiers. When the last casualties had been attended to I nearly fainted, and found, to my surprise, that it was already 4 p.m. I realised that I had not yet had breakfast. Feeling miserable and exhausted, I left the clinic and found to my dismay that my room had collapsed. With no bed to rest on and no clothes to change into I was close to tears. Then a knock brought me to my feet. The chief cashier stood at the door looking rather sad.

"Miss Lim, our cow has been killed by the Americans." Doris burst out laughing.

"Don't tell me that the Americans came all that way just to kill your cow."

Not long before the chief cashier had asked me if I would like to join him in buying a cow as milk was so difficult to get. The particular cow he had in mind cost eight hundred guilders and four of us contributed to this sum. When our cow arrived she was honoured by a large crowd of people who turned out to welcome her to the factory. She looked wild and vicious and I had doubts as to whether I could manage her. She was housed in an *atap* hut behind the clinic and every fourth day it was my turn to take her out grazing. The cow and I trod slowly through the village and sometimes past the office of the factory. The Japanese would pop their heads out of their office and smile, while the coolies called out cow girl. However, I did not mind because I thought that I would soon get some milk, but alas, the long-awaited milk never seemed to come, although the seller had sworn when we bought her that she was in calf. I shed tears when the cashier told me of this casualty. Later the carcass was divided into four portions and we had meat to eat for weeks on end.

Many unexploded bombs lay scattered all over Indareong. Surprisingly, the factory was not much damaged, but enough to put it out of action for a few weeks. The harbour suffered more, as a ship loaded with cement had received a direct hit and there had been many casualties. The bombing had also damaged all the water pipes in the village and for a while we had to carry water from the mountain streams. The Japanese were determined to get the factory in working order quickly. They searched for labourers in all the villages, even those as far off as Sawah-Loento, and within a short period four thousand coolies were brought to Indareong. They were very unhealthy, and many of them had dirty sores and ulcers all over their bodies. It was a tedious enough job to get them clean, let alone to keep them well. Slowly the damaged pipes and houses were repaired and the fear of another attack seemed to disappear; but Doris and I did not discount the possibility for we thought that the Allies would surely come back as soon as they knew that the factory was in working order again. The Japanese knew that the Allies were keeping a close watch on it. "Cement is very important in war," one of the Japanese told me, a fact that had never occurred to me. Doris suggested that we should resign from the clinic as soon as we knew that the factory had been repaired, but I told her that we would need a good reason for resigning.

There were persistent rumours in Padang that the military police had a black list of people suspected of being Allied spies and we did not want to get on to it. Doris agreed; she lived in terror of being taken for a spy, because she had seen what happened to spies in China. I made some inquiries through friends to find out whether our names were already on the list. Apparently they were not. However, Doris was not satisfied and said that she would try to think of some scheme which would enable her to leave Indareong.

Personally, I was happy there. I had interesting work to keep me occupied and I thought that if I were going to be killed it might as well be at Indareong as anywhere else. Apart from the noise and the dust of the factory, Indareong stood in lovely surroundings. Moreover, I liked the villagers though their carefree attitude worried me. They would not work if they had enough to eat for the next day. For instance, one day I met the father of a family wandering aimlessly around the village and I asked him why he was not at work. He told me proudly that he had won a few guilders at cock-fighting and he reckoned that the money would last his family for some days, so he was taking a rest. I scolded him.

"Don't you ever save? Suppose you should become ill and be unable to earn. What would happen to your children?"

He smiled. He had enough money for a few days and that was all he cared about.

As time went on conditions became more difficult. Food was hard to get and expensive, so Doris and I decided to keep poultry. We each bought a pair of geese and ten chickens and, in addition, I bought fourteen ducks. I had no idea how to choose them. When the flock of ducks arrived I noticed a fat one which I was told by the owner would soon lay eggs. Actually it had a tumour and was well on its way to the grave. When I fed them I noticed two of them standing aside waiting for the rest to finish feeding. The seller said that these were male ducks and had been taught to behave like gentlemen! I was furious when I discovered that one was lame and the other blind. The blind duck was always left behind by her companions and when she discovered it quacked loudly. Doris used to tease me and say that I should take my ducks to a circus. Week after week I waited for them to lay eggs but gradually one by one the chickens and ducks disappeared. They either died or they were eaten by snakes. Most of these snakes were harmless but one day I saw a large one swallowing a goat. Afterwards it went to sleep and I informed the police who killed it and to my annoyance dumped the carcass near the clinic.

The sound of sirens became quite usual in Indareong but there was no more bombing; in spite of this Doris grew more and more afraid and she begged that we should leave soon. Then suddenly one day she decided to marry a Chinese.

I was amazed and said, "Doris, have you any love for him?"

She looked at me in a queer way and answered, "Don't be stupid, Janet. I have no love whatever for him. I only want to get out of this place."

Argument was useless. Afterwards she pleaded with me.

"Janet, I need your company. I cannot stay alone with a man day in and day out; if I loved him it would be different. Do come with me, please."

What could I do? Doris and I had few other friends, so finally I decided to go with her. She told the Japanese authorities that she was getting married and that I was her adopted sister and that she would like me to come with her. I felt that the Japanese doubted that the marriage was a genuine one, but finally they gave permission for both of us to go.

On 28 October 1944 we left the cement factory by truck with our chickens, geese and two dogs.

The farm which belonged to Doris's husband stood about three miles from Indareong. It consisted of one small *atap* hut though a new house was being built. When we arrived we all shared a tiny room, sleeping on the cement floor; to add to our misery it rained all day and the two dogs refused to sleep outside. We had to cook all our meals in the open and before beginning to cook had to gather firewood and leaves. We visited our half-built house daily until we were told that it was impossible to complete it because of the shortage of materials. In spite of this, we decided to move in.

The house shook and swayed and only one room and a verandah were usable. We had to stoop low to enter our front door, and the back door leading to the kitchen was so narrow that, thin as I was, I had to walk sideways to get through it. When it rained the mud in the kitchen was ankle-deep so we often cooked in the open under an umbrella. The main problem was to find drinking water near the new house. Daily we searched fruitlessly and dug the ground and by the evening we were exhausted. Then one day Doris's husband returned with a beaming smile. A short distance away near the edge of a *padi* field he had dug a hole about two feet deep and had found water. Indeed, there was plenty of water, but so muddy that it was not even fit for washing. However, we got a large tin and filled it with sand, to serve as a filter, and though the water was by no means clear it could, after being filtered many times, be used for drinking. Around this waterhole we built an *atap* fence so that we could take our baths there. Soon afterwards Doris and I set to work to clear the grass around the house. When we had finished a storm broke out and swept our enclosure and the kitchen away. Exhausted, we looked at each other.

"It's hopeless, Janet. Oh, why did we leave Indareong?"

It was the first time I had seen Doris in tears; perhaps it was from misery because we no longer seemed to be civilised beings. We wore sarongs without blouses, no shoes, and ate out of banana leaves.

After we had been in the place about a month, living on our savings, our money and provisions were nearly exhausted. The vegetables we had planted were too young to be edible and the man's wage was insufficient to keep all of us alive. Then Doris had an idea; there were still four thousand coolies in Indareong and the Japanese supplied them with food. She thought if we could contact the Japanese and contract to supply them with vegetables bought direct from the farmers we should make enough to keep ourselves. The Japanese agreed to the scheme and we set to work. Three times a week we rose early and waylaid the farmers as they came down from the hills on their way to the market. We bought everything they had and sold it to the Japanese at a good profit. One morning when we were sitting on the roadside waiting, some of our friends passed by and exclaimed, "Good heavens, what has come over you two?"

Embarrassed we looked away. Our shoes we kept for going to Padang, and the muddy water had stained all our clothes. Unfortunately our buying and selling of vegetables soon came to an end, for the cement factory, which had been partially put out of action by bombing, was repaired and then fewer coolies were needed.

Our farm was infested with mosquitoes and I did not have an adequate net. I soon contracted malaria and every second day I was in bed with a high temperature. The only medicine I had was quinine tablets which made me very deaf. Slowly I became weaker and weaker till it was agony to move about and work on the farm. Finally I could only do the housework, and the planting and digging had to be done by the other two. One day my temperature was higher than usual, my face became swollen and painful, I had difficulty in swallowing and I realised that I had a throat and ear infection as well as malaria. Luckily just then two Japanese doctors from the Padang Hospital came to the farm and saw me. Dr Nakanura had been educated in the United States and had practised in Japan; the other, Dr Suzuki, had worked in one of the rubber plantations in Malaya before the war. They immediately took me down to the Padang Hospital where I was admitted into the woman's ward and stayed for two weeks. The two doctors then tried to persuade me to work in the hospital, but I said that I would have to talk it over with my friends on the farm. Fortunately I was able to convince Doris that I was a burden to them and that here was an opportunity to earn my living elsewhere. I added that I would come back to the farm for the weekends and share my salary with them. This seemed to satisfy her. I was not sorry to leave. Apart from everything else, there were frequent quarrels between Doris and her husband.

A storeroom near the wards was given to me for a bedroom until I could find accommodation elsewhere. The hospital, called the "Roemah Sakit Besar" (big sick house), stood outside the town; it was the one I had visited when I was at the Yamato Hotel. Different sections were used by the military and the Japanese civilians, and there was a women's and children's ward which was in the care of Malay doctors and nurses. I was detailed to the Japanese civilian ward under Drs Nakanura and Suzuki; I was the only Chinese nurse working in the hospital. All the prescriptions, medical reports and instructions were written either in Malay or in Japanese which put me at a great disadvantage, so that I could only serve the meals, tidy the wards and do the dressings.

The Japanese patients were difficult to nurse. The tuberculous ones spat anywhere they pleased, although sputum mugs were supplied and they had been instructed how to use them. One afternoon I found a TB patient cleaning his mouth in the kitchen sink and I told him not to do it. He was very angry, "Japanese nurse, no tell patients what to do. You,

China, go away." I decided to be brave and reported these patients to the Japanese doctors. They told me to wait in their office while they went to see the patients. What they said I do not know, but after this I was put into the X-ray department, where I was kept busy all day, except when work was interrupted by visits to the air-raid shelters. Bombers often circled round, but the Japanese had great confidence that the Allies would never bomb a hospital. The doctors were very pleasant to work under and gave the same treatment to all nationalities. They had many Chinese and Malay friends who often came to them for help. Some drugs were impossible to get outside the hospital but these people seldom went away empty-handed. These two doctors earned the goodwill of the population and I am glad to say that when I visited Tokyo in 1954 I saw Dr Nakanura in good health; I do not know what happened to Dr Suzuki.

As I could not cook in my room, arrangements were made for me to collect my daily ration from the kitchen—it consisted of a bowl of rice and a piece of meat as tough as leather. Although I was working in the X-ray department I had constant contact with the women's ward and, in particular, I came to know many patients who were comfort girls. They had weekly medical examinations for venereal disease outside the hospital and if infected were sent in for treatment. I grew to understand their difficulties and problems well, and this knowledge gave me more sympathy for a similar group whom I cared for after the war when I was a nurse in the Government Social Hygiene Hospital in Singapore.

I still continued to have attacks of malaria and often I felt very weak.

"Janet, wake up, it's time to go to work," my roommate called to me one morning.

"I don't want to go to work today; I feel awfully tired. Please tell the doctors." Then I shouted after her, "No, wait for me; I will come."

When I arrived a Malay boy ran towards me, saying, "*Nona*, your friend Doris die."

"Don't be silly, I saw Doris only the day before yesterday; she is more alive than you are."

Then someone called out, "She has been murdered."

"My God, the Japanese have done it."

"No, her sweetheart."

I ran towards the ward. I was told she was not there.

"She is over there." A nurse pointed to the mortuary. Doris dead? I could not believe it. Then as I went to the mortuary door, I began to imagine what had taken place. The day I had left the farm there had been a violent quarrel and her husband had threatened to kill her. But it had never entered my head that such a thing could happen. We washed her body. There were seven knife wounds and the doctors told me that she had died of peritonitis from her abdominal wounds.

I could not go back to the farm to get her clothes, so for her burial we dressed her in one of my dresses; this horrified many superstitious people in Padang. A rough cheap coffin arrived and, on the same afternoon, it left the mortuary carried by two men, with my roommate and me as the only mourners. There was no service, only a cross to mark her grave. Before we left the burial ground my roommate warned me not to enter anybody's house for the people were very superstitious. As soon as we reached our room she packed her belongings for she feared that the ghost of Doris would appear to me. She left for good!

In obedience to Chinese custom I wanted to visit the grave on the third day, but the burial ground was in a prohibited area. It was under strict military control and one had to obtain special permission to go there. Fortunately, the two Japanese doctors were able to accompany me. The grave was a pathetic sight for the rain had washed the earth away and the coffin was clearly visible. While the doctors wandered off to look at some of the other graves, I sat there thinking. I had witnessed many deaths yet how few of these people had been prepared to die. Doris did not want to die; she had left Indareong to avoid dying. My father wanted to live so that he might see me grow up. Many whom I had seen die were terrified of death. I myself had been close to death several times and each time deep in my heart there was a certain fear— fear of the unknown—for my conception of life after death was then vague and uncertain. During my school days I had studied the Bible and been to Sunday school and I had gathered that if a person was good he would go to heaven, and that if he wasn't he would be sent to hell and stew in everlasting fire. When I had thought that I was near to death I had prayed very hard, not for the safety of my body, but for the salvation of my soul. Yet I thought that if only I had remembered the security I had had in the village in China in my father's love, perhaps that would have helped me to understand more about God's love and care.

A month later I had a letter to say that I must make a statement in court. The courtroom looked like a concert hall. There were rows and rows of benches with a table at one end of the room and behind this a platform for the officials. The court was crowded with people, all Chinese. A Malay "judge", an interpreter, two Japanese officers and Dr Suzuki sat on the platform. Two Chinese approached me and told me very nicely that I must not say anything to get Doris's husband into trouble. I said, "I have nothing against Doris's husband; he has been good to me, but I am here to tell everything that I know."

Just then Doris's husband came in escorted by two policemen. He burst into tears when he saw me and said, "Janet, I am sorry."

At the end of the trial he was convicted to three years' imprisonment. Immediately a loud howling and wailing arose in the courtroom.

I asked, "Why are you all crying?"

"If the people make a lot of noise the judge will think that the convicted man was good and had many friends," came the reply.

This device certainty produced the desired result, for the prisoner was now told that if he behaved well he would only have to serve one year's sentence. Feeling more sorry than ever for Doris, I returned home.

Two weeks later, two men whom I had never met came to see me. They said that they were working and living near the burial ground and that at night they heard Doris calling for help. At first nobody would believe them, but now everyone in the neighbourhood seemed to have heard her! They said that Doris cried on Tuesdays and Fridays from midnight to two o'clock in the morning! I was very upset and did not know what to do, until an elderly Chinese suggested that we should hold a service at the graveside. He said that Doris, who was a Roman Catholic, was evidently not satisfied because she had been buried without a proper service. So a service conducted in Malay was held at the graveside, attended by seven people of whom I was one. No more weeping was heard after that.

As the months went by, more and more planes were seen around Padang and sometimes we remained in the air-raid shelters for hours on end even though few bombs were dropped. Soon there were rumours that the end of the war was near. In June most of the Japanese civilians were called up for further military training. Some Japanese whom I knew well told me Tokyo had suffered badly from Allied bombing, but their countrymen were determined to fight to the last.

Still, the rumours must have affected Japanese morale, because one day when I was in a trench I overheard a Japanese and a Malay make the following remarks: "B29 very big; look how low the plane is; anyone could shoot it."

"Best not to anger them or else they might drop a few bombs here."

I thought to myself that if the Japanese were afraid of annoying the

Allied bombers, then the end of the war could not be far off. That was a pleasant thought. Another indication that the war was ending was the increasing friendliness of the Japanese towards me. One day I met a Japanese who came alongside me and fell into step with me, and said, "Lim-san, what do you think of the Japanese people?"

"What do you mean?" I answered cautiously.

"Well, we have all heard that the Japanese Kempetai treated you badly when you first arrived in Sumatra."

"Then of course I hated them, but time heals the wounds. Now I have forgiven them but it is difficult to forget."

We both smiled and bowed.

One morning in August the local press reported that the Americans had dropped a very large bomb on one of the islands of Japan, causing heavy casualties. The paper said that its use was severely criticised by neutral countries. We all wondered what sort of bomb it could have been.

I was in the Oes' house when I heard the first rumour that the Japanese had surrendered. The rumour was true but it was days before the news was given out officially. I could not believe my eyes when I read that the war had come to an end. Indeed I was too dazed to feel either happy or sad. Amongst the local population there was unrest. The Indonesians did not want the Dutch to return; some said to me, "We want our freedom; we have been slaves long enough." People gathered in groups whispering and plotting, but the Japanese were now too busy with their own plight to take any notice. The Chinese minority were the most uneasy of all, because they feared that they would be attacked by the Indonesians. And now I realised that the end of the war had brought new problems almost as difficult as the old.

Because the Japanese were selling all they possessed, prices became chaotic. The staff of the hospital were given double pay plus nine yards of pretty dress material. Many families gave farewell dinners to Japanese friends; the latter drank, sang and were merry. Next day some of them died by committing hara-kiri. One man who failed to kill himself in this way was brought into the hospital when I was on duty. He was sent to the operating theatre where his gaping abdominal wound was stitched up, but he died of peritonitis two days later,

"It needs great courage to die such an honourable death," one of the Japanese patients told me. "You hold the knife firmly in your right hand, stab it into the left side of your stomach and draw it towards the right. Then the knife is raised to the neck and the carotid arteries are cut. Many people lose their nerve when they see their intestines and faint without giving the fatal cuts to the arteries."

Daily, lorry-loads of local men returned from the forced labour camps. Some had not seen their families for years and there were many happy reunions. Meanwhile, the Japanese were busy preparing comfortable quarters for their own internment camp! I could not make up my mind what to do. The Oes wanted me to remain with them until the Chinese New Year. I was still working in the hospital. One morning two planes circled round Padang bringing food for the internees. Two large barrel-like drums containing food were dropped; they were from the Australian Red Cross. The people of Padang were amazed. One of them said to me, "The white men must love their people very much."

Then two European officers called at the hospital to arrange accommodation for sick internees. I had not spoken to white men for a long time and their appearance seemed so strange to me that I was on the point of running away when they saw me.

"Hallo, Nurse, do you speak English?"

"A little." I hesitated; I had almost forgotten the language because its use had been forbidden.

"Could you please make us some tea?"

I put a tray in front of them. They came back the next day.

"Nurse, you make very good tea—real English tea. Now don't run away; please join us, Are your parents here?"

"No, I am from Singapore."

"You are British, one of our own people." He held my hand firmly. "How do you come to be in Padang?"

"It is a long story and it is so hard for me to tell you in English."

They thanked me for the tea and left.

A great number of ex-POWs were taken to Padang and were housed in a large building guarded by two sentries. By wearing my nurse's uniform and a Red Cross armband I was able to gain entrance and take things to them. In this way I found many of my former friends from the SS *Kuala*. Some of them were unrecognisable for they had become so very dark and thin. One of them said to me:

"Janet, you look no better than we do. Why are you so thin?

All I could tell them then was that I had had continuous attacks of malaria. It was late when I left.

Next morning when I went on duty I was surprised to find that the wards which had previously been full of Japanese patients were now filled with British men and women. Some were very ill; all had lost weight. They were very hungry and, in spite of being warned of the danger of overeating, they ate plateful after plateful of rice. The two Japanese doctors visited them regularly and the internees had a good opinion of them.

On 17 September when I went on duty the ward was empty. As I did not know what was happening and had no work to do I wandered about aimlessly until I met an officer who told me that all the patients had gone to Singapore. When I heard this, I felt very homesick and burst into tears. The officer was surprised and asked me why I was so upset. I told him that my home was in Singapore. He replied that if he had known this he would have sent me back with the patients. Then he told me to report to his headquarters at the Yamato Hotel. Three days later I called at the hotel and was interviewed by a major who said to me: "You will leave this afternoon."

"Not so soon," I cried. "Please let me say goodbye to my friends."

"All right, but you must be quick, as there are only going to be one or two more flights to Singapore."

Parting does not come easily to me. I had spent three years in Sumatra. Now I could only think with gratitude of the Malays and even of the Japanese who had helped me in my difficulties, and above all I thought of the Chinese who had helped me, often at great risk, with gifts and encouragement. It was they who had given me confidence in myself and instilled in me the determination to carry on. I had experienced the bitterness and brutality of war, yet my chief memory at that moment was not of this, but of the acts of kindness and sympathy I had received from both enemies and friends. These I shall never forget.

On 22 September 1945, I left Padang in an RAF Dakota. My faithful friends, the Oe family, were there to bid me farewell. This was the first time I had been in an aeroplane, so I was allowed to visit the cockpit. As I was admiring the beautiful view from the pilot's cabin, I suddenly heard a cry: "Singapore."

Acknowledgements

In 1949, I spent a holiday in Thailand. The war was fresh in my mind and I told my friend, Mr Allan Chin-Bing, some of my war experiences. He suggested that I should write something describing my adventures and that is how this book began. During 1949 and 1950, I wrote parts of the chapters dealing with the first few months after the surrender of Singapore and Mr Chin-Bing kindly helped me to revise the material. For various reasons, chief among which was my departure for England in 1951, the story was not finished and the text was left untouched till 1955.

By 1955, the publication of a war story seemed a little belated and I had given up the thought of finishing the book. Then Dr C. Keys Smith, Medical Officer in Charge of St Andrew's Mission Hospital, Singapore, urged me to go back to my manuscript and, because of my rather unusual experiences as a young girl, he suggested I should begin the story with my childhood. I am deeply indebted to Dr Keys Smith for checking the historical facts surrounding my life, for helping to correct my English and for continued encouragement. It was due to him that the book was completed. I am also very grateful to his wife, Catherine, who has given me much help and who also typed out the first draft.

My thanks are due also to Mrs Anne Wee and Miss Jean Waller for helpful criticism. Mr W.A. Spreadbrow, who was with me on the raft during the evacuation of Singapore, kindly lent me a diary of his which covered this period. A number of other friends have made useful comments on certain sections of the book about which they had special knowledge.

I would also like to thank my publisher Philip Tatham for his patience and understanding, John Suan and Hilda Lee of St Andrew's Mission Hospital, Noraini Bakri of St Margaret's Secondary School, Jeff Howarth of Anti-Slavery International, Teri Liew and Hana Schoon of Keppel Corporation, Joy Seah, Lim Kheng Chye, James Nunn for the cover design, and my son Michael and his wife Eleisha.

Finally, I am indebted to the Reverend Canon R.K. Sorby Adams who so willingly agreed to write the Foreword. It was written a few days before he left Singapore on his retirement. He had been a missionary in Singapore since 1927—a period which covered the whole of my life there.

The names of some of the people mentioned in the book are fictitious, and if there should be any resemblance to persons, living or dead, bearing these names, this would be purely coincidental. Some place-names have also been altered or omitted. But the story is true and alterations have only been made where it was desirable to hide the identity of some of the people involved.

Needless to say, the friends who have helped me are not responsible for what I have written. The story is my own, though I would not have dared to put it in writing without their help. As I wrote and tried to recapture and record the feelings and ideas of my childhood I often smiled at my youthful immaturity. But the chief conviction that came to me was a renewed sense of gratitude to all those who have helped me. To them, I shall always be thankful.